Joan is a seasoned prophetic voice in the Body of Christ. I love the design of her first book, which has a creative, blessed mix of personal testimony, scriptural teaching, and actual prophetic words received by Joan over the years. Joan's effort enriches us all. I'm looking forward to her next book!

Bruce Latshaw
Senior pastor at The Barn Vineyard Church
Landenburg, Pennsylvania

Surely one of the greatest gifts and privileges that our Father God bestows upon His sons and daughters is the gift of his voice and vision, so that we may know His way and partner with Him in the advancing of His rule and reign in all creation. He entrusts us with His secrets and what the intentions and plans of His heart are for us personally as well as for all who dwell on the earth. This volume of writings, given to us by a tested and trusted prophet, will encourage you greatly in your walk with God, and also assist you in turning your own heart to hear God's voice.

I first met the author, N. Joan Huth, when she visited my church over ten years ago as a member of a team of students from Dr. Randy Clark's Global School of Supernatural Ministry. Her love for the church, her clarity in sharing the revelation of all that God brought to her, and her encouraging heart, made a deep impression on this senior pastor who had encountered a number of people in my ministry who desired to be recognized as prophets, but seemed to be more critical of the church in their expression of their gift rather than loving. Since that weekend at my church, I have now become the

Director of Education of the school where Joan became a graduate, and my continued encounters with her have always been encouraging, strengthening, and above all, expressing the love of the Father in Jesus Christ. Joan is a faithful woman of God, a teacher, equipper, and prophet, and all she brings forth encourages, exhorts, and builds up the body of Christ.

Hear His Voice, Follow His Way flows from the heart of the Father through the heart of a daughter who has given her life to be a blessing to the entire church. As you read each of these gifts of revelation that God has given Joan, you will encounter His love, His desire for you, and you will receive a fresh impartation of hope for whatever season of life you are experiencing. Jesus made it clear that those who are His sheep will be able to hear and recognize His voice, and will be able to follow His way (John 10:27). May you encounter this good Shepherd in these powerful words.

Dr. Mike Hutchings, Director
Global School of Supernatural Ministry, Global Certification Programs
Global Awakening, Mechanicsburg, Pa.

Follow
HIS WAY,
Hear
HIS VOICE

Follow
HIS WAY,
Hear
HIS VOICE

N. Joan Huth

XULON PRESS

Xulon Press
2301 Lucien Way #415
Maitland, FL 32751
407.339.4217
www.xulonpress.com

© 2019 by N. Joan Huth

All rights reserved solely by the author. The author guarantees all contents are original and do not infringe upon the legal rights of any other person or work. No part of this book may be reproduced in any form without the permission of the author. The views expressed in this book are not necessarily those of the publisher.

Unless otherwise indicated, Scripture quotations taken from the New King James Version (NKJV). Copyright © 1982 by Thomas Nelson, Inc. Used by permission. All rights reserved.

Printed in the United States of America.

ISBN-13: 978-1-54567-392-8

Table of Contents

Chapter 1: My Journey 1

Chapter 2: Energizing your Prayer Life 16

Chapter 3: A Short Study on the Prophetic 60

Chapter 4: Receiving the Gift
of Prophecy and Using it 71

Chapter 5: Judging Prophecy 95

Chapter 6: You are God's Mouthpiece 103

Chapter 7: Prophetic Intercession. 110

Chapter 8: God's Wisdom in Scripture. 115

Chapter 9: Angels in our Midst 139

Chapter 10: Having Ears to Hear 142

Chapter 11: God Is Calling His Church
to a Great Awakening 150

Ending Remarks 183

About the Author.......................... 185

INTRODUCTION

No one thinks it is unusual when someone makes a new discovery. We might find some things astonishing, but they are readily accepted because they come from the world. When it comes to hearing the voice of God, most people would deny this could ever be. In fact, many in the church do not believe He still speaks to His children today. However, it was normal for God to speak to Adam and Eve as He walked and talked with them.

Genesis 3:8-10 says, And they heard the sound of the Lord God walking in the garden in the cool of the day, and Adam and his wife hid themselves from the presence of the Lord God among the trees of the garden. Then the Lord God called Adam and said to him, "Where are you?" So he said, "I heard Your voice in the garden, and I was afraid because I was naked; and I hid myself."

We see it was normal to have a conversation with God. The Lord and Cain had a direct conversation in Genesis 4:8–18. We could go on and on, with Noah, Abraham, and all through the Old and New Testament. It was and is now normal for God's children to hear His voice. It is essential for God's children to hear His voice. He wants to speak to every one of His children on an individual basis. To accept this as normal, we must not allow the world's views to hinder us. We hear Him through our faith in Jesus Christ. Christians are new creatures in Him, and we can hear from our Lord through His Holy Spirit who lives in us. The power to hear from the heart of God belongs to us. We should expect to hear God's voice; if we do not expect to hear Him, we will not know it is His voice we are hearing.

The information in this book contains knowledge I have acquired by studying God's word and walking in the gift of the prophetic. As you seek God for understanding the gift of prophecy, remember the words of Paul in First Corinthians 14:1, "Pursue love, and desire spiritual gifts, but especially that you may prophesy."

Chapter 1
MY JOURNEY

Several years ago, I heard God ask me to write a book about my experiences in prophetic ministry. It has been resting in my spirit ever since. Every now and then, I would think how I would like to share what God had done in my life but never had a conviction or urgency in my spirit to go forward with what I thought was just a suggestion from the Holy Spirit. Now I know it was not just a suggestion but a calling to step out in faith and obedience in what God has asked me to do for His glory. Many books have been written on the gift of prophecy, and I always felt my knowledge could not contribute any more than what had already been written. But God's ways are not my ways. He told me it is time to put my experiences into print and that I am not to consider this book as one that is in competition with any other. This book will present His wisdom to all who desire to know the living God and to hear His voice on a personal level.

It is out of obedience to God that I decided to go ahead and act on what I have been hearing. My desire is that all who hold this book in their hands would have a deeper understanding that God is a personal God who wants to communicate with His children on a one-on-one basis. Many hours of preparation of seeking the Holy Spirit for His guidance have gone into this manuscript. I must add it was not a chore, nor do I consider it a work that I needed to accomplish for my self-esteem. It was a joy spending time with the Holy Spirit who is the composer, and I am just the receiver to give God's message to encourage His people. I pray you will receive what God has for you as the Holy Spirit imparts His Wisdom in your spirit. May you be blessed abundantly. Deuteronomy 8:3c states, "Man shall not live by bread alone, but man lives by every word that proceeds from the mouth of the Lord."

I am sure there are more than one hundred ways to get a message from God, as He communicates to each one of us in so many different ways. This book is meant to help you hear from God personally, wherever you are. He is always speaking in ways you can understand. I pray this book will help you hear God's

My Journey

voice to follow His way on your journey with Him into your destiny!

If I were to write the story of my thirty-plus years of knowing Jesus Christ, I am sure I could write pages and pages. Therefore, I asked the Holy Spirit to highlight stories that would encourage and touch the hearts of all who read this book. I would like to begin by giving my testimony, which started in January, 1981.

In 1979, I had a back injury that caused me a great deal of pain. After living with that pain for two years, I decided to take the surgeon's advice and have an operation to remove the herniated disc that was the cause of the problem. A friend suggested I attend an Episcopal healing service. I know now it was the Holy Spirit drawing me.

Attending that service was the beginning of a whole new life for me. On the night of January 21, 1981, I accepted Jesus as my Lord and Savior. I had never heard the message of being "born again" even though I had attended church most of my life. My life was totally changed in one night. I left the healing service, knowing God had touched me, and I wanted to know more about the wonderful feeling I had inside. Just two weeks later, praising God with a Bible in my suitcase, I had back surgery and have been free from back pain ever since.

God started to work in my life immediately. In a matter of two months, I attended a Bible study and started going to a Spirit-filled Episcopal church. It was the start of my new life in Christ. God was so good to send me to a charismatic Episcopal church, a denomination I was familiar with and could teach me how to live my new life in Christ.

My heart was eager to find more of God. I couldn't get enough of His Spirit; I would attend at least two healing services a month where I learned more about the gifts of the Spirit. My hunger to know God grew daily. I would look for every chance to find a quiet place, so I could read the Bible and seek Him in prayer. Within weeks, I began to hear God's voice. I know now it was because I was seeking Him with all of my heart, and He was drawing me closer through His Spirit. I cannot explain how I knew it was God, only that it was His peace I was experiencing. I began a journey of pursuing God that would change my life forever.

In the first six months of being born again, I began to journal what I was hearing from God. I heard the words in my spirit and began to write them down. I didn't stop to analyze if it was God, the devil, or my own words; I knew the Holy Spirit was keeping me safe from doubt and fear. As I continued to journal what God said to me, the enemy occasionally tried to bring doubt and confusion into my mind, but as I prayed that my mind and heart would be clear, I felt the peace of Jesus and knew what I was hearing was from God's heart. I know now this was part of the learning process.

The more you step out in faith, the more confidence you receive, knowing you are hearing His voice and not your own thoughts.

John 10:1-5 says, "Most assuredly, I say to you, he who does not enter the sheepfold by the door, but climbs up some other way, the same is a thief and a robber. But he who enters by the door is the shepherd of the sheep. To him the doorkeeper opens, and the sheep hear his voice; and he calls his own sheep by name and leads them out. And when he brings out his own sheep, he goes before them; and the sheep follow him, for they know his voice. Yet they will by no means follow a stranger, but will flee from him, for they do not know the voice of strangers."

Maturing in the Gift

I will always remember the love and acceptance I felt in my home church during those first days of following Jesus. God's presence filled the atmosphere;

it was truly like walking into heaven. I experienced the meaning of worshipping God like never before as I lifted my hands, praising the Lord. I was so in love with Jesus, and I surrendered completely to Him. One Sunday during worship, I felt an awakening in my spirit that took over my whole body. I did not understand what was happening to me, but I knew it was God. I heard words stirring in my spirit—words that I knew were from Father God. I felt like I either had to open my mouth and say what was bubbling up in my spirit or blow up. So, to my surprise, the Holy Spirit opened my mouth and out of my mouth came His Words. It went something like this, "I love you, My children, and pour out My blessings on you today."

After speaking God's message, I felt a release in my spirit as His peace filled my entire being. Although my personality was not what I would call bold at that time, I did not care what anyone thought; I was so caught up in the Spirit that I let the Holy Spirit have His way. That was the beginning of learning to be obedient to the Holy Spirit and letting Him have His way with what I would later learn was called the gift of prophecy.

My pastor recognized God had given me a gift to speak to His people and encouraged me to speak as I followed the leading of the Holy Spirit. As a result, he

My Journey

allowed me to grow in the gift of prophecy God had given me. God's words flowed through me on a regular basis during our Sunday services. I would be shaken inside with the manifestation from Holy Spirit, but I was never truly comfortable when eyes were on me as I prophesied what the Holy Spirit wanted me to speak to God's people. Obedience in surrendering to the Holy Spirit overtook my timidity. God's encouraging words were profound as He spoke comforting words to His people. However, my pastor shared with me some of the comments made during a meeting with the elders of the church: "Why don't you shut that woman up! When she speaks, her message is always centered on how God loves His people!"

My pastor told me his reply was, "She is growing in her gift, and I have given her permission to speak as Holy Spirit leads her."

First Corinthians 14:3 says, "But he who prophesies speaks edification and exhortation and comfort to men." This seems to be a good place to have you ask the Holy Spirit to take you back to the first time you knew it was God you were hearing. Ask Him to help you to remember the peace and tranquility you felt as you experienced the overwhelming presence of God that captured your heart in a way you had never felt before. We were born to be in God's presence and to know that He is always with us and desires us to hear His voice. Father God loves to talk to His children just as He talked with Adam and Eve and just as Jesus heard His voice as He walked on the earth!

Everyone hears God's voice. He breathed His breath into us when we were created; we hear from God through our spirit, spirit to spirit. Genesis 2:7 says, "And God formed man of the dust of the ground, and breathed into his nostrils the breath of life and man became a living being." God is Spirit; the breath He breathed into man is His Spirit. If God imparted His Spirit into man, then we are of His Spirit. Therefore, not only does He hear us, but He expects us to hear from Him.

Jesus tells us in John 5:19, "Most assuredly I say to you, the Son can do nothing of Himself, but what He sees the Father do; for whatever He does, the Son also does in like manner." We can know what the Father is doing in our lives because Jesus lives in us. Therefore, we can hear, feel, and sense His love. The Holy Spirit causes our spirit to come alive, to be aware of a holy God, our Creator. We are called children of God and are able to hear His voice clearly because we are washed clean with the shed blood of Jesus Christ. We can communicate with our Father God because we are one with Him in Spirit and in truth through His Son Jesus.

Jesus is the key to recognizing God's voice, and the Holy Spirit is the activator. The Holy Spirit delivers God's voice to our spirit where He gives us discernment to apply it to ourselves or to whom it is to be given. There is no way to explain this in the natural; we can discern it only in our spirit and not by our own intellect. All this is done in and through Holy Spirit in Christ Jesus, our Lord and Savior.

John 14:16, "And I will pray the Father and He will give you another Helper that He may abide with you forever the Spirit of truth, whom the world cannot receive, because it neither sees Him nor knows Him; but you know Him, for He dwells with you and will be in you."

John 14:26, "But the Helper, the Holy Spirit, whom the Father will send in My name, He will teach you all things, and bring to your remembrance all things that I said to you."

John 15:26, "But when the Helper comes, whom I shall send to you from the Father, the Spirit of truth who proceeds from the Father, He will testify of Me."

God's Wisdom in Scripture

Prophetic Words are written in this italic font.

Romans 8:16 says, "The Spirit himself bears witness with our spirit that we are children of God."

How is it that My children are frightened to speak My Words? Is it because of the lack of understanding that My children are My own? Ownership in this case is not ownership to control to the point of making you My puppets but to give you direction for your own good. To respond to My Spirit that works through you in prophecy is to give you the very words from My heart. The promises I have made to you cannot be erased but can only be increased as you portray My will in your lives and cling to what is good, what is holy, and what is pure. Allow Me to make the decisions of the gifts I will use through you, for in this way the Spirit will indeed testify that you are My children.

Mark 7:14–15 says, When He had called all the multitude to Himself, He said to them, 'Hear Me, everyone, and understand: There is nothing that enters a man from outside which can defile him; but the things which come out of him, those are the things that defile a man."

What is said here, My children, is very true. For it is that which you prepare in your heart that goes forth for others to see and hear. Is it a good thing that comes from your Father when My Spirit testifies through My words when I have chosen to speak through you? Is it a good thing that I wish to use you who are acceptable in My sight because of the whiteness of the robe of Jesus Christ? Do not think I would stray from you as you seek this gift or think that you are not suitable to speak My words. To do lip service to Me and not complete the works I have prepared for you is not a good choice. Do unto Me as I do unto you; that is to listen to My voice as I listen to yours and touch the body of Christ with the heavenly shower of the voice of God.

People who have not received Jesus as Savior still hear God's voice but do not recognize it. Their spirits have not been awakened by being born again through the sacrificed blood of the Lamb, Jesus Christ, the one and only Son of God. When we receive Jesus as our Savior, He opens our spiritual ears to hear God's voice through His Holy Spirit. Think about how you were born again; it was not by your own strength but only as you surrendered to God in seeking Him.

John 3:5–6 states, "Most assuredly, I say to you, unless one is born of water and the Spirit, he cannot enter the kingdom of God. That which is born of the flesh is flesh, and that which is born of the Spirit is spirit."

John 14:17 states, "The Spirit of truth, whom the world cannot receive, because it neither sees Him nor knows Him; but you know Him, for He dwells with you and will be in you."

Word of the Lord

I long to come into the hearts of all I created to hold them and nurture them, so they would feed on who I am to make them peace makers and lovers of who I am. I want them to see themselves as they are inside Me.

I am full of wonderful and beautiful things, and I want My world and My creation to know and experience who I say I am. Then all will be at peace when they know I am God, their God!

You Hear God's Voice in Every Part of Your Day

To get on with my story, I cannot express how passionate I was when I came to know Jesus was alive and that God cares about me and loves me just as I am. The more I searched for God, the more I wanted of Him. I attended church for most of my life but did not know God personally. I began to wonder why I had to wait for so long. I quickly put the past behind me and knew God was with me no matter what my past and that this was a new day in Him. I knew in my heart, as I keep my eyes on Jesus, God would lead me into my destiny. Psalm 121:5–8 states, "The Lord is your keeper; the Lord is your shade at your right hand. The sun shall not strike you by day, nor the moon by night. The Lord shall preserve you from all evil; He shall preserve your soul. The Lord shall preserve your going out and your coming in from this time forth, and even forevermore."

Praise God for a pastor who chooses to mentor and nurture his sheep. When I look back on the days when I was a baby Christian and how my pastor nurtured me in the gift God gave me, I am amazed at how much it impacted my life by being obedient and allowing Holy Spirit to have His way. I would like to encourage you to rest in what you are hearing from God. As you are hearing His words of comfort and direction in your spirit, allow yourself to relax and let Holy Spirit continue to complete His message. What He has to say will bring you comfort and peace. God will never condemn you or fill you with fear. He will always comfort you.

Second Timothy 4:2–4 states, "Preach the word! Be ready in season and out of season. Convince, rebuke, exhort, with all longsuffering and teaching. For the time will come when they will not endure sound doctrine but according to their own desires, because they have itching ears, they will gather for themselves teachers; and they will turn their ears away from the Truth, and be turned aside to fables."

Prophetic Word

Truth will always be heard, along with My wisdom and knowledge, among My children.

Forever I will encourage My ones to speak as I lead them to speak. I will prepare them for any journey, any counsel, or any encouragement that is needed to gather more children for My kingdom. I ask only that first they must allow My Spirit to judge their hearts in order to hear clearly My words of righteousness. If My children do not hear My voice, to have them pursue My will, they in turn will listen to others who do not want the ways of God. Then they will listen to man and his judgment of what will be said. To listen for My voice is likened to the coolness of a breeze on a summer day. Would I not refresh you, My children? For I wish to hold you closer so the enemy will not entice you to stray.

Chapter 2

ENERGIZING YOUR PRAYER LIFE

*I*t is an honor and a privilege to come before the throne of God, with Jesus as our intercessor. We, as the body of Christ, should look at our prayer life occasionally to see if it is not only pleasing to God but also if we are using our prayer life to its fullest potential. God tells us we are more than conquerors in the name of Jesus. (Romans 8:37).

I find it awesome that God not only speaks to us through His written Word but also through His prophetic word. Everything God says to us must be confirmed through His written Word. All the glory belongs to God and not man. God must receive all the glory and honor as the body of Christ goes forth in this world to serve and love Him.

Here are some scriptures to encourage you:

Romans 8:35, 37 states, "Who shall separate us from the love of Christ? Shall tribulation, or distress, or persecution, or famine, or nakedness, or peril, or sword? 37 'Yet in all these things we are more than conquerors through Him who loved us.'

Hebrews 4:14–16 says , "Seeing then that we have a great Priest who has passed through the heavens, Jesus the Son of God, let us hold fast our confession. For we do not have a High Priest who cannot sympathize with our weaknesses, but was in all points tempted as we are, yet without sin. Let us therefore come boldly to the throne of grace, that we may obtain mercy and find grace to help in time of need."

Ephesians 2:4–9 states, "But God, who is rich in mercy, because of His great love with which He loved us, even when we were dead in trespasses, made us alive together with Christ [by grace you have been saved], and raised us up together, and made us sit together in heavenly places in Christ Jesus, that in the ages to come He might show the exceeding riches of His grace in His kindness toward us in Christ Jesus, for by grace you have been saved through faith, and that not of yourselves; it is the gift of God, not of works, lest anyone should boast."

We Are Called to Be Prayer Warriors

We, as Christians, are the only tool God has on the earth to tell the world about Jesus Christ, God's only begotten Son, who came to the earth to free all from Satan's demonic treachery. (1 John 3:8) How can we go forth and be God's servants, His messengers, as He has asked us to do? We are at war with an enemy that is unseen but known to us all. His name is Satan, which means great adversary, enemy, or foe, but God gave us a powerful tool in prayer. May God help us to be the prayer warriors we need to be! I ask that you search your heart as you read the following prophetic word that I feel is a timely utterance from Holy Spirit. God is asking us to come to His throne to receive more of Him and more of His divine revelations as we fill the heavens and the earth's atmosphere with anointed Holy Spirit prayers in these last days. As God's children penetrate the heavens, He hears our prayers, for the prayers of a righteous man avails much. (James 5:16)

Prophetic Word: Energizing Our Prayer Life

There is much to get ready for in these days My children, for the darkness is showing itself in plain view for the world to see. As this starkness holds its power over the weak, their conditions will spill over into society, and many will be pulled into the blackness that seeks no return to light. The world will bring its own judgment upon itself and then there will be nowhere to turn but to God, the Creator of all things. I ask My children to heed My call for a richer prayer life. I have planted in your hearts the richest knowledge of My kingdom and have provided you with the Spirit's leading to go and be My messengers. Will you not seek Me in what I have to give you in the times ahead for a deeper relationship with Me?

I am the giver of your faith, the provider of your joy, and the defender of your cause for Christ. My Son stands with outstretched hands with tears of sorrow for the world.

He stands steadfast to be your companion so that you draw closer to Me just as the first disciples and as He devoted Himself to prayer to hear the will of His Father. I ask you to be closer to Me than ever before, for the world's struggle for survival is slipping fast. Do not let go of My hand, for in these days of trouble, you are to stand in the gap for those who are unable to stand for themselves. Do not grow weary; depend upon My strength for no mountain is too high when the Spirit's wind carries you to the top in My rest.

HOW DO WE PRAY?

Before we go any further looking at our prayer life, let's ask the Holy Spirit how you can go deeper in your intimacy with God our Father through prayer. You might start by asking God to reveal anything that is blocking you from having your prayer time filled with the Holy Spirit's power. Expect to receive the answer as you spend time with Him. It would help if you would start a journal. Pour your heart out to God and write down your deepest thoughts. Make a commitment to sit and have your time with God with the Holy Spirit. He is the only one who can mold and shape us into what God wants us to be. I have found if I allow the Holy Spirit to guide me in my prayer time, I have the satisfaction that I have prayed all I needed to pray. If you go by your feelings and emotions, you might feel you have forgotten someone or feel you have not directed your prayers in the right way. Do we need a set format to present our petitions to God? It is easy to get into the habit of following a ritual in our prayer time, such as having our prayers written down on a piece of paper or always starting our time with God in the same way. It is a good thing to do something fresh and new when coming to God in prayer.

The Holy Spirit can and will do that very thing for you. I speak from experience; I would go to God with a typed prayer list, going down the line one by one. My flesh was satisfied that I finished the whole list, but as I recall, I did not always have peace in my spirit. I started a new approach to God in my prayer time by asking Holy Spirit to guide me in my prayers. It took a while to feel comfortable, but as I relaxed with the Holy Spirit, I could feel the difference. I released many prayers on my list to God and realized the flow of what I was praying gave me peace and complete satisfaction that God was hearing my prayers. Presently, there are still times when I feel I need to write down what I'm expecting God to do as I decree and declare the Word of God over what I am praying for, calling those things that are not as though they were. (Romans 4:17)

As I pray, I declare the scripture that pertains to my prayer request and use my authority in the name of Jesus instead of speaking words of the flesh.

As you seek God's wisdom on energizing your prayer life, here are some basic guidelines that will help:

Value Your Sources

a. Jesus: Come to the throne of God by His authority.
b. Holy Spirit: Allow Him to be guide in the name of Jesus.
c. The Bible: The Word of God is your best source.
d. A journal: Be ready to listen for God's voice and how He will speak to you on a personal level.

These Will Be Your Goals

a. To receive all God has for you in your time of prayer
b. To feel comfortable praying with the Holy Spirit
c. To know Father God waits with expectancy for you to come to Him in prayer

Structure to Remember

a. Allow enough time to come to the throne of God and not feel hurried.
b. Come expecting to hear from God.
c. Enter God's presence with praise and thanksgiving.
d. Believe the importance of having a one-on-one relationship with your Father God and how He waits for you to seek His face.

God wants to prepare your heart to hear Him in a new way. He wants you to come into a deeper understanding of knowing who He is and His purpose for your life in Christ. I pray God will penetrate your heart as you seek His way to energize your prayer life so that you will receive the full benefits of being a child of God.

James 1:5 tells us, "If any of you lacks wisdom, let him ask of God, who gives to all liberally and without reproach, and it will be given to him."

Prophetic Word: I Wait with Expectancy

> The point of all Godly teachings is to reach the understanding of how the hearts of My children are bound to My heart in completeness and oneness in the Spirit realm. When two hearts are bound together as one, they are grieved when they are apart from one another. The love I seek from My children is a love that can only be truly recognized in My Spirit. This is a love that has been called into being because of My desire to be in fellowship with My children and to have them respond with the same desire to fellowship with their Father.
>
> I sit on My throne, seeing the needs and desires of My children as they have a fondness of wanting to serve Jesus Christ in their lives. However, many have forgotten

Energizing your Prayer Life

My grace as we fellowship together. Instead our fellowship has become a distant dream because they have allowed the duty of the world's time to drift them away from My throne. Forgetting the real nature of their beginning, they instead reach poor reasoning to do better as they try on their own. All I want is to welcome them with the ease and happiness that they will feel when My grace abounds to them as we meet and bring our hearts together as one. There is a trust that comes when the foundation of glory meets with a child of God. When the quality of desire is the same between us, then expectancy is the purpose for both. This brings unity and destroys all things that try to break the bond that is eternal.

I have shown you the way to My kingdom, and you have responded with joy that fills your hearts. I ask that you use your joy to believe I will bring forth the desires of your heart. I ask that you be united with Me as My child and come to me in holy surrender. The fortunes of the kingdom have much to do with the battle that rages in the world. It is not likely that the world will accept one who is convinced, through the showing of their life, that God is willing to fellowship with them.

I give My children all understanding and knowledge as they come to Me with open hearts. I wait with expectancy to give you a glowing promise that will increase your commitment and bring you to the full desire of discipleship. In your hearts, remember to think of your God as the pleasure you have always looked for. As you come to Me with Jesus holding your hand, the light from His face will light your path, and you will be gently lifted to My throne.

PRAYING WITH HOLY SPIRIT

Psalm 49:1–4 says, "Hear this, all you peoples; give ear all inhabitants of the world, both low and high, rich and poor together. My mouth shall speak wisdom, and the meditation of my heart shall give understanding."

Prophetic Word

The true form of all things is in My hand. I give to those who are truly seeking My wisdom and knowledge. If I give freely to My children who are discerning My truth, in the Spirit of truth, will I not gladly enrich them with the heart of the truth-giver? Will I not take enjoyment over My children who chose Me over the world? I am in the midst of My children and have full charge of them as they surrender to Me. I will fill the hearts of those who are living by My Spirit. These are days filled with distasteful fruits from those who are giving from their flesh. I am asking you, My children, to discern with the wisdom of My Holy Spirit what is of flesh and what is of My Spirit. Will you not consider what I have said to you in My Word? Seeking My kingdom through My Spirit will bring you far more in the light of knowledge than searching with your flesh. I do not come to you today to be a forgetful voice but to be an anointing that will fall upon you that will reap much as you are a blessing to others.

To stand for Christ is to stand with God as your only embellishment and not the world's approval. To be a disciple of Christ today is like a tree laden with fruit that is standing in the middle of a barren land, a land that shuns the likes of this fruit because of a God that calls the world to holiness. You, My children, are filled to overflowing with My Spirit. Do not allow your fruit to spoil for lack of use, for the results will only end in disappointment for you. I have chosen you to accomplish My plan. Each of you is called to a purpose. Your willingness to live in My Spirit calls you to a new identity for all to see.

Living for your God demands much obedience and sacrifice, but I ask not of you what I will not do for you. There will be much to see through My Spirit in these days as I have prophesied. See the fulfillment of My Words and be a working part of My body.

Feed on My Word and enjoy the fellowship of My Spirit. There are many rich days ahead for you. I am your God who loves you, and what I enjoy most is to bless My children. There is happiness in My presence, so allow My Spirit to flow and meet with Me each day at my throne of holiness.

BEING LED BY THE HOLY SPIRIT

How can you get ahead of the devil? How can you see what he is up to before it happens? Keeping your connection open with God will keep your spiritual discernment sharp. How we get the connection is through God's only Son, Jesus Christ, who will change your life completely and forever if you let Him. This can be accomplished if you walk in the Spirit and not the flesh.

Romans 8:5–6 states, "For those who live according to the flesh set their minds on the things of the flesh, but those who live according to the Spirit, the things of the Spirit. For to be carnally minded is death, but to be spiritually minded is life and peace."

We must give control to the Holy Spirit by faith. It takes practice, as no one is perfect. If we want to please God, He will make it easy.

To keep ahead of the enemy, we must be in constant agreement with the Word of God. When speaking the Word of God, we will see that which is impossible turn into victory. This does not come automatically; it comes with prayers and supplications to God in the mighty name of Jesus. Victory comes when we allow the Holy Spirit to lead us in warfare. He gives us discernment between good and evil and encourages us to pray the Word of God.

John 14:16–17 tells us, "And I will pray the Father, and He will give you another Helper, that He may abide with you forever, the Spirit of Truth, whom the world cannot receive, because it neither sees Him nor knows Him; but you know Him, for He dwells with you and will be in you."

THE HOLY SPIRIT SPEAKS

Would we open our ears to listen; would we open our eyes to see? Would we sit still and hear if Holy Spirit stood right here and said to you and me, "Let Me introduce myself. I'm the Holy Spirit standing here in full view; oh, don't look so surprised. I'm a real person just like you. You might call Me your look-alike, your double so to speak, I have feelings and emotions just like you. I've come to live inside your heart, and I can see all you do.

The Holy One, our Father, wants you to know He put me in your temple so that you would grow to maturity to be just like His

Son. I, Holy Spirit, came that you might know Him. I came in the Father's Son Jesus's place that He might continue to walk this earth through you as your heart is open to Me. God wants all to see Jesus through each and every one of you. I, Holy Spirit, live in your temple. Now you are holy! Let me give you an example:

I, Holy Spirit, am now your eyes and ears. I give you the compassion that Jesus knows and feels. Yes, now you have ears to hear and eyes to see, just like the Father. Remember, because you have Jesus in your hearts, that makes your spirit holy. That's the way it will always be! When you feel your heart and spirit stirring, that is my clue to you to pay attention to what I am saying; the Father has something for you to say and do. He is stirring me in your spirit, so be awake and alert. I am Holy Spirit, so please do not turn away. You might miss giving God's blessing through me to someone during any part of your day.

Energizing your Prayer Life

I, Holy Spirit, fill you to the fullest if you only care to be. I am holy, which now makes you holy; the Father declared it so. It is I, Holy Spirit, I and no one else who makes the holy words clear, so you can rely on them not only for others but to hold them true for yourself. You see, I am the Holy Spirit; no one can compare to me. I am the one who stirs up the gifts inside you; the gifts the Father placed there. I am Holy Spirit and my responsibility is to show you what Jesus would have you do. Your gifts and talents were specially placed within you to make you who you are; the Father wants you to know what they are.

Just ask me, and I will tell you. I have not hidden them, so you will not know. It is a privilege and an honor for you and only you to know God's Spirit—that is, me! Open your ears, eyes, and hearts, and let us go and speak the truth. Jesus is calling you; hear Him clearly say; "My dear children, hear the Holy Spirit's voice; honor Him and be true to Him. This is the Father's way."

Prophetic Word: Hearing Is By My Spirit

I have put the voice of My Spirit in your hearts. He is the only one who can guide you to be more like Jesus Christ. It is through the truth in My Word that you will learn of Me. Only My Holy Spirit can turn your prayer life into a richer experience. By being led by My Spirit you will touch a dying world that does not see the truth of the living God. You play a needed part in the world that is leaning toward the way of man and his understanding and holds no truth in its Creator but only a false truth of his own making.

Seeking My way is seeking the way of Jesus Christ. This is the only way that will lead you to My will and the destiny I have chosen for you. Happiness is truly when My Word prevails in your life and when you put Jesus above all else. Will you be in union with Jesus who will never fail as you join Him in the everlasting knowledge that comes when *you allow Him to intercede on your behalf? Faith is hearing Jesus in My Word of faith. Truly I ask you to come; come and seek what the world cannot give you. Seek true wisdom from My heart as you come to Me through the blood of the Lamb that was sacrificed for you, My beloved children.*

Hebrews 7:25 states, "Therefore He is also able to save to the uttermost those who come to God through Him, since He always lives to make intercession for them."

Ephesians 2:4–7 states, "But God, who is rich in mercy, because of His great love with which He loved us, even when we were dead in trespasses, made us alive together with Christ (by grace you have been saved), raised us up together, and made us sit together in the heavenly places in Christ Jesus, that in the ages to come He might show the exceeding riches of His grace and His kindness toward us in Christ Jesus."

First Corinthians 15:58 states, "Therefore, my beloved brethren, be steadfast immovable, always abounding in the work of the Lord, knowing that your labor is not in vain in the Lord."

Romans 8:35, 37–38 states, "Who shall separate us from the love of Christ? Shall tribulation, or distress, or persecution, or famine, or nakedness, or peril or sword? 37-38, 'Yet in all these things we are more than conquerors through Him who loved us. For I am persuaded that neither death nor life, nor angels nor principalities nor powers, nor things present nor things to come, nor height nor depth, nor any other created things, shall be able to separate us from the love of God which is in Christ Jesus our Lord.'

HINDRANCES TO OUR PRAYER LIFE
UNCONFESSED SIN

Psalm 66:18 states, "If I regard iniquity in my heart, but Lord will not hear."

First John 1:9 states, "If we confess our sins, He is faithful and just to forgive us our sins and to cleanse us from all unrighteousness."

CONFESSION OF SIN BRINGS US
CLOSE TO GOD

Second Chronicles 7:14 states, "If My people, who are called by My name will humble themselves and pray and seek My face and turn from their wicked ways, then will I hear from heaven and will forgive their sin and will heal their land."

James 5:16 states, "Confess your trespasses to one another, and pray for one another, that you may be healed. The effective, fervent prayer of a righteous man avails much."

INSINCERITY:

Matthew 6:7–8 states, "And when you pray, do not keep on babbling like pagans, for they think they will be heard because of their many words. Do not be like them, for your Father knows what you need before you ask Him."

UNBELIEF:

James 1:5–8 states, "If any of you lacks wisdom, let him ask of God, who gives to all liberally and without reproach, and it will be given to him. But let him ask in faith, with no doubting, for he who doubts is like a wave of the sea driven and tossed by the wind. For let not that man suppose that he will receive anything from the Lord; he is a double—minded man, unstable in all his ways."

PRAYING WITH FAITH:

Matthew 17:20 states, So Jesus said to them, "because of your unbelief; for assuredly, I say to you if you have faith as a mustard seed, you will say to this mountain, 'Move from here to there,' and it will move; and nothing will be impossible for you."

Mark 11:23–24 states, "For assuredly, I say to you, whoever says to this mountain, be removed and be cast into the sea, and does not doubt in his heart, but believes that those things he says will be done, he will have whatever he says. Therefore I say to you, whatever things you ask when you pray believe that you receive them, and you will have them."

Hebrews 11:6 states, "But without faith it is impossible to please Him, for he who comes to God must believe that He is, and that He is a rewarder of those who diligently seek Him."

HAVING YOUR TIME WITH GOD

Do you come to God in prayer to receive all you can from His bountiful supply of grace? Do you remember all of His promises and how He waits with an expectant heart to hear your needs, so He can give you those promises? Our wish tank can overflow, and He will continually empty it and fill it again with His blessings.

Prayer is allowing our relationship to grow in the knowledge of our Lord. How can we come to know Him if we do not spend time with Him? To know God and His love and to feel the peace of His warm Spirit within us, we must fellowship with Him. God wants us to spend quality time in prayer, so He can fill us with a deeper love for Him, not only to enrich us, but to use us to present our Savior, Jesus Christ, to a lost and dying world.

RELATE TO GOD WITH ALL HONESTY

"Some men's sins are clearly evident, preceding them to judgment, but those of some men follow later. Likewise, the good works of some are clearly evident, and those that are otherwise cannot be hidden" (First Timothy 5:24–25). We can be trapped by our own conviction, but God sees all that is in our hearts. The obvious sin is sometimes the most difficult to ask forgiveness for. It is usually the sin that has us compromising with the world, one that we are comfortable with because we have not heard the Holy Spirit's convictions but instead listen to our own convictions. Psalm

139:1–3 says, "Oh Lord, you have searched me and known me. You know my sitting down and my rising up;; You understand my thought afar off. You comprehend my path and my lying down, you are acquainted with all of my ways.

Feeling a false protection of confidence will bring us further and further from the Spirit's conviction. Why would we run away from our inheritance that brought us freedom from sin? God wants us to live in freedom. Trying to flee from God by accepting false accusations from our flesh will only keep us from submitting to Him and from His presence. The Holy Spirit will bring us to the cleansing of the cross and therefore we need a closer relationship with Him as we walk daily in His presence.

Second Corinthians 5:20-21, "Now then, we are ambassadors for Christ, as though God were pleading through us; we implore you on Christ's behalf, be reconciled to God. For He made Him who knew no sin to be sin for us, that we might become the righteousness of God in Him".

Ask God to lead you in the Spirit and consider:

Romans 8:26, Likewise the Spirit also helps in our weaknesses. For we do not know what we should pray for as we ought, but the Spirit Himself makes intercession for us with groanings which cannot be uttered.

Now He who searches the hearts knows what the mind of the Spirit is, because He makes intercession for the saints according to the will of God.

Psalm 69:5 states, O God, You know my foolishness; and my sins are not hidden from You.

As we lean on God, we will know what His purpose is for our entire lives. We begin to trust God when we receive Jesus as our Savior. Then, as we grow in our Christian life, we yield more and more and allow Him to take over. We must always strive never to give up what Christ has for us as we run the race.

Philippians 3:12–14 states, "Not that I have already attained, or am already perfected, but I press on, that I may lay hold of that for which Christ Jesus has also laid hold of me Brethren, I do not count myself to have apprehended; but one thing I do, forgetting those things which are behind and reaching forward to those things which are ahead."

COMING TO GOD IN PRAYER WITH A RIGHT ATTITUDE

Psalm 44:20–21 states, If we had forgotten the name of our God, or stretched out our hands to a foreign god, would not God search this out? For He knows the secrets of the heart.

Jeremiah 12:3 states, "But you, Oh Lord know me; you have seen me and you have tested my heart toward You."

Psalm 19:14 states, "Let the words of my mouth and the meditation of my heart be acceptable in Your sight, O Lord, my strength and my Redeemer."

God will process thoughts in your heart when you desire to please Him. When you want His will and not your will to be done, you can make your heart right with Him. All God asks is that you yield to Him, and He will take care of the rest. "There are many plans in a man's heart, nevertheless the Lord's counsel that will stand." (Proverbs 19:21).

Prophetic Word: I Call You To Be Ambassadors

Finding the way to My truth is a call that is strong in the hearts of My children. I am touching you, My children, with the truth you are searching for. If you desire to identify with Me, your God, and with all power, it will be subsequent to the way you continue

Energizing your Prayer Life

to follow My Spirit. In the world there is a need to have direction to know the fullness of life. It is a time when there are many new directions to take to find the truth of life. The deceiver calls to the emotions of man because he knows this is where the heart of those who want goodness in the flesh look for answers.

It is the little ones for which My heart cries. These are the little ones who are indeed breaking the Commandments I have called them to obey. This is due to the lack of responsibility of their nurturing families. How can I say to you, My children, to stand guard against the enemy for these little ones who are so needing the prayers of My people? I have asked not only through My prophets, but also through the direction of the elders of the church to tend to the church in My holy direction. It is not only through those who have the ministry of directing My church that I asked to go forth, but to every one of My precious children whom I love and with whom I want to share My wisdom.

I now ask you, who are called by My name, who are striving for My purpose, to serve Me and serve Me well to be the ambassadors I have called you to be. My voice calls louder than ever before. This is a time when the power of My name will be so evident for the world to see. Jesus is the owner of all that is to come. Watch, My children, for this is the holiest of times to be seen in My church. My love is pushing you to My fullness. My hope is in this love that is necessary for My church to have to be ready for the wind of My Spirit that is coming in such force that it will astonish even those who are familiar with My power. My voice speaks to My church and is loud to hear if only My children would come to Me in prayer with open hearts.

Lean on Me, My children, and know that I care and will satisfy your dreams and visions as I have given them to you. Hold on tightly in these days, My people, for these are days that will take your full commitment for My purpose to be realized in My church.

SPIRITUAL WARFARE

Ephesians 6:12 states, "For we do not wrestle against flesh and blood, but against principalities, against powers, against the rulers of the darkness of this age, against spiritual hosts of wickedness in the heavenly places. Therefore take up the whole armor of God that you may be able to withstand in the evil day, and having done all to stand."

First Samuel 17:47 states, "The battle is the Lord's."

COME TO THE THRONE WITH PRAISE AND THANKSGIVING

Casting Down the Strongholds of Satan and Building Up the Strongholds of the Kingdom

Focusing on praise and worship will add to the clarity of God's stronghold in our lives and will pull down the stronghold that is trying to take our eyes off God's promises. When we allow the enemy to penetrate our minds with negative thoughts, this opens the door of our soul to take captive those thoughts and causes a block in our spirit, which prevents us from hearing the voice of God through the Holy Spirit. All sin and disobedience come from our thought life first. When we make a choice to walk in the Spirit and not the flesh, it then becomes natural for God's children to reject the lies that Satan tries to plant in our minds.

Second Corinthians 10:3–6 states, "For though we walk in the flesh, we do not war according to the flesh. For the weapons of our warfare are not carnal but mighty in God for pulling down strongholds, casting down arguments and every high thing that exalts itself against the knowledge of God, bringing every thought into captivity to the obedience of Christ, and being ready to punish all disobedience when your obedience is fulfilled."

When we rebuke the enemy's influence and hold onto the hopes we have as born-again believers in Jesus Christ, not only can we claim the victory, but others will see our witness and be drawn to Jesus. Many are doomed with their thoughts and are dragged down in defeat because they are deceived by Satan and his constant attempts to follow the flesh and not the Spirit of the living God.

First John 4:4 tells us, "You are of God, little children, and have overcome them, because He who is in you is greater than he who is in the world."

It is essential that we, as the children of God, be ready to hear God's wisdom. Therefore, as we continue to walk in the Spirit, we will not be vulnerable to react to Satan's attempts to have us follow our flesh. Matthew 26:41 says to, "Watch and pray, least you enter into temptation. The spirit indeed is willing, but the flesh is weak."

Jesus tells us in John 10:1–5, that He is the shepherd of His sheep:

"Most assuredly, I say to you, he who does not enter the sheepfold by the door, but climbs up some other way, the same is a thief and a robber. But he who enters the door is the shepherd of the sheep. To him the doorkeeper opens, and the sheep hear his voice and he calls his own sheep by name and leads them out. And when he brings out his own sheep, he goes before them; and the sheep follow him, for they know his voice. Yet they will by no means follow a stranger, but will flee from him, for they do not know the voice of strangers."

So, what is spiritual warfare? Spiritual warfare is being on constant guard against the enemy and his tactics. It is praising God in times of blessing and also in times of need. Warfare in the Spirit is pressing in when we do not feel like it; it is putting on "the oil of joy for mourning, the garment of praise for the spirit of heaviness; that they may be called trees of righteousness, the planting of the Lord, that He may be glorified." (Isaiah 61:3)

USE YOUR AUTHORITY

What is the meaning of authority? The dictionary defines authority as "the power or right to give orders and enforce obedience; the power to influence others based on recognized knowledge or expertise; an authoritative person, book or other source." Jesus gave His disciples authority to use His name against the enemy, Satan. This can be seen in Luke 10:19, which says, "Behold, I give you the authority to trample on serpents and scorpions, and over all the power of the enemy, and nothing shall by any means hurt you." It is no different now than it was when Jesus first spoke these words. We have the delegated power of Jesus Christ within us, who is the power. The Holy Spirit guides us. He is our director. The devil must submit to God's power within us; that is the way it is; and that is the way it will always be.

Ephesians 6:10 states, "Finally, my brethren, be strong in the Lord and in the power of his might."

As we call on the power of Jesus, the power of God that we carry within us, we will see victory over the enemy. We do not rebuke the enemy by our own strength but by the power in the name of Jesus.

As I have walked with Jesus as my Savior these many years, I have found there must be a constant renewing of my mind. It is necessary, not a choice, to use the authority we have in Jesus Christ because of the world in which we live.

"You are of God, little children, and have overcome them, because he who is in you is greater than he who is in the world." (1 John 4:4)

As we ponder over the Scriptures that tell us about the authority we have in the name of Jesus, the Holy Spirit will bring them to our remembrance as we pray. Only the Word of God can teach us and change us into who we are in Christ. God has given us His power to use, so we can live the life he has called us to live.

John 10:10 says, "The thief does not come except to steal, and to kill, and to destroy, I have come that they may have life, and that they may have it more abundantly."

Jesus released us from the power of Satan when He died on the cross for all mankind. When we, Christians, acknowledge this truth and receive Him into our lives as our Savior and Lord, we also receive His power against the enemy. As we grow in the knowledge of who we are in Christ, the desire to fight against Satan becomes more of a reality. Yes, God will fight for us; He will answer our prayers, but He also expects us to use His power by the words we speak in the mighty name of Jesus, His Son.

Prophetic Word
Have No Fear Of The Enemy

As I call you, My children, to come to My throne and gather My words of encouragement, I also want to fill you with the full understanding of who you are as a child of God. The pure and satisfying refreshment of My Spirit longs to prepare you to receive more of My glory. In My full and most loving way, I want to support you in your visions from Me so that you may live your lives to the fullest.

Even in general conversation, I want My children to be aware of what they speak. My ears are always open, not only to hear you speak, but also I listen to what you are saying. As you focus on how Jesus would handle each situation, My Spirit will speak the words that hold My truth.

My presence within you has a quality voice to speak but can only do so as you recognize that you represent a mighty God whose presence lives inside you. I have called you to be My representative, My ambassador, to all the world. It must not be looked upon as a duty but as a privilege to be a representative for Jesus Christ who holds all power and all honor in My created world.

My church holds authority through the name of My Son; therefore, it is beyond the power of Satan to overrule the name above all names. As My Spirit calls My church to act against the enemy, He is allowing My will to be shown that will glorify My name. Those who know their position in Christ will use their authority to glorify Jesus and will not show fear of the enemy. There must be a willingness to be transformed from fear to boldness, from lack of knowledge to the wisdom of the Spirit. Without the knowledge of the Word of God, there is no power to change things. How can one have something if they do not know its substance?

These are days of uncertainty for the world. If they, who do not know Jesus, continue to stumble and fall because of the works of the enemy, it will lead to devastation to the point of no return. I am calling My church to see the nakedness of the people of the world, so they might have compassion for the lost. Truly, truly, I say to you: Use your authority in the name of Jesus, who rules and reigns in your life. Speak clearly and distinctly to Satan, using your God-given authority, Jesus Christ. Remember to be willing to use My Word in all you do, and all will go well with you, My beloved.

Prophetic Word
Place My Values Above The World

I hear the words of my children as they lift up their voices in the clearness of My Spirit. It is My eternal pleasure to touch all lives. I have words of vitality from the goodness of My heart for you to give to all who would hear.

To trust in a God, who is making your life what He wants it to become, is not easy in the flesh. I have much to say to you for the trust I ask in return. Many have needed answers yet have not asked because of the many disappointments of the world around them. There are more who hear the sounds of an unstable world than those who hear the expectations of My kingdom. It is possible to transfer lost hope to the abounding hope of the kingdom that truly holds all good values. Placing the world's values above heavenly values will end in losing hope of ever receiving answers from a Father who cares for all I have created.

If the hearts of My children are focused on My Spirit, the natural inclination will be to offer prayers to the throne, expecting a response. When My children pray with their old nature, their hearing is distant and strained. For My children to reach the heights of hearing Me beyond any doubts, there must be a unity between us in our relationship wrought by an attitude that wants to please their God in every way. This will always bring My natural response, which is a blessing that will give Me all of the glory.

Jesus Christ brings the infilling of the Holy Spirit. Anyone who feels their God is a God who shows no justice to their prayers will find a division between themselves and their God. Promises are not to be taken lightly in My Word, for I speak them with clarity and expect My children to be firm in their belief and pure in their acceptance of these promises. A pure heart knows when it is their Father who speaks and will tell the testimonies of the blessings they have received. Knowledge comes to the heart of the believer.

This is the knowledge that speaks of a God who gave His Son, Jesus Christ, to bless all because they have believed in Him. Would I, your Father, deprive you of anything that *is good for you? I ask you today to deliver a message from the kingdom that will stir the hearts of many. Say to those who will listen, "The heart of God lives in His Word that lives today; Jesus is the Word. He is the answer to all dreams and desires. Quality of life is to believe Jesus loves His children and will satisfy them with the pleasures of His kingdom."*

JESUS CALLS US TO BELIEVE

John 16:23 says, "And in that day you will ask Me nothing. Most assuredly, I say to you, whatever you ask the Father in My name He will give you."

Hearing these words of Jesus to the fullest measure is only possible through the Holy Spirit. How can we match this truth with any argument that comes from the world? In the name of Jesus, our Father hears us and expects us to come to Him with our needs. How can we, as God's holy children, deny Him our wishes? Even though we face the enemy in our everyday lives, this should not deter us from our faith in what we know is God's truth in His Word.

Receiving the words of Jesus will bring us closer to the fact that we can only grow in our faith as we believe in God's Word. Believing Jesus is the key to God's heart is in Scripture.

John 14:13 says, "And whatever you ask in My name, that I will do that the Father may be glorified in the Son." Jesus has stated this precious promise simply. Our faith soars when we read these Words of Jesus, mounting up to the heights of God's throne, as high as the Spirit can go.

John 16:24 says, "Until now you have asked nothing in my name. Ask, and you will receive, that your joy may be full." We receive the joy of God's promises when we offer up our prayers through the righteousness of Jesus, knowing He hears us because His Word speaks truth. Continued prayer brings continued joy. Lifting our request up in a prayerful attitude will fill us with the pleasure of knowing our God hears our petitions.

Matthew 18:20 says, "For where two or three are gathered together in My name, I am there are in the midst of them." Can our prayers be far from God when Jesus gives us His strength through His presence? Without Jesus's true compassion, His love for us, we would not survive in our own hopes. The truth of salvation proves it is only through the blood of Jesus Christ that we can be sure God receives and will answer our prayers. God sees us as His children when Jesus holds us up to Him.

JESUS IS AS REAL AS YOU WANT HIM TO BE

Picture yourself in a sailboat in the middle of the sea. The wind is still. The sound of the water lapping against the sides of the boat is the only sound you hear. You are wondering how you will make it to the shore without the help of the wind in your sail. You are waiting for the wind to come and carry you where you cannot take yourself.

Think of your life in the spiritual realm. How is it possible to know God's direction without allowing Him to take you by the wind of His Spirit? Living in Jesus Christ is total submission to Jesus through the Holy Spirit. How can the children of God be complete unless we are walking in the Spirit? Walking in the Spirit allows Him to cleanse, change, and direct our lives as we open our hearts to receive the fullness of God.

To reach the fullness of Christ as we live on the earth, we, His children, must be in total submission. This calls for dying to self. After being washed in the blood of Jesus, the old nature becomes subject to the new, becoming fully submissive to the Holy Spirit who came to take authority over the flesh. When our flesh tries to dominate our lives, this causes a battle that rages between spirit and flesh. When this happens, we hear voices other than the Holy Spirit.

How do we relinquish our flesh and give complete charge to the Holy Spirit? Instead of picturing yourself in a sailboat sitting still for lack of wind, envision waiting for God's guidance and listening for His voice. Be ready for the wind of the Holy Spirit to move you in God's perfect will and timing. God's truth in you longs for the fullness of Christ to be manifested.. It is the Holy Spirit that says, "Call on Me, for Christ calls you to draw closer to Him through Me."

While waiting for the return of Jesus, God calls us to go forth to touch the world for Christ. How can the power of God be still in us if we allow the Holy Spirit to spread His fire before us? All we must do is to be obedient to His voice. As we go forth in our prayer time with God, let us be determined to follow the Holy Spirit's direction and flow in His attitude of love and joy. God loves us as we are. As we desire more of Him, He will desire more of us.

Psalm 37:3 says, **"Delight yourself yourself also in the Lord, and he shall give you the desires of your heart."** "t

Chapter 3

A Short Study on the Prophetic

The Gift of Prophesy

*W*e speak prophecy through the faith that comes from the confidence we have in Jesus Christ through the Holy Spirit. In order to use this gift of prophecy, we must first believe God wants to speak to His people. If we hold any doubts that God wants to speak to us, He will not be able to use us to the fullness of our destiny.

If we feel the call of the Holy Spirit telling us we have the gift of prophecy, beyond the gifting we receive when the Holy Spirit comes to live inside us, we must develop this gift. There are people you and I will meet, who will not be able hear what God wants them to know

A Short Study on the Prophetic

except through us. Therefore, we should be open for the Holy Spirit to use us at His will.

Romans 12:6 says, "Having then gifts differing according to the grace that is given to us, let us use them: if prophecy let us prophesy in proportion to our faith."

I am not saying that God cannot reach people in other ways or that you and I are the only source by which this person may hear God. God speaks in many ways. Of course, we who are born again in Christ know God speaks to us through His Word. Prophecy can never replace the Word of God which is essential for everyone to know who claims to speak for Him.

The Holy Spirit can speak into every aspect of our lives. God knows our comings and our goings, our thoughts and actions. When He cannot get our attention one way, He will try another. We have dreams and visions while we sleep, so God can get our attention without interruptions.

The pattern is like this: We hear from the Holy Spirit and He gives us discernment, we process what we are hearing through the Holy Spirit's direction, and then we speak what we are hearing. We may need to hold onto what we are hearing until we know it is time to act on what God is saying. We always wait on the Holy Spirit's timing.

How do you act on what you know God has given you? What do you do with this gift, and how do you know to what length God wants to use this gift in you? Ask God. He wants to use you through the confidence you have received, which is your faith in knowing He speaks to you. You will hear Him because He who lives in you is greater than he who lives in the world. You are the temple of the Holy Spirit; therefore, when He speaks, you will hear. The Holy Spirit has ways of getting our attention. He knows we want to hear from our God who loves us. Trusting the Holy Spirit is a minute-by-minute learning experience. Anyone who is a disciple of Jesus Christ can vouch for that. We all have our Holy Spirit stories and how He has drawn us closer to God. (1 John 4:4)

Old Testament Prophets and New Testament Prophets

Old Testament Prophets were chosen by God to be His direct messengers. It was an anointing that God chose to give to an individual. God spoke through the Old Testament prophets. They called themselves servants of God, guardians of Israel, and watchmen. Amos 3:7; Jeremiah 7:25; Isaiah 62:6; Jeremiah 6:17; Ezekiel 3:17.

Once a prophet knew he was called by God, he dedicated himself wholeheartedly to the calling. They were usually under the authority of a king. (Haggai 1:13; Malachi 3:1)

New Testament Prophets:
Pentecost: Holy Spirit Fire

As children of God under the New Covenant, we have the Holy Spirit within us to represent God our Father in and through Jesus Christ, who is our Savior and Lord. Jesus spoke to His disciples in Acts 1:8, "But you shall receive power when the Holy Spirit has come upon you; and you shall be witnesses to Me in Jerusalem, and in all Judea and Samaria, and to the end of the earth."

On the day of Pentecost this promise was made available to us. Acts 2:1–4 tells us, "When the Day of Pentecost had fully come, they were all with one accord in one place. And suddenly there came a sound from heaven, as of a rushing mighty wind, and it filled the whole house where they were sitting. Then there appeared to them divided tongues, as of fire, and one sat upon each of them. And they were all filled with the Holy Spirit and began to speak with other tongues, as the Spirit gave them utterance."

As it was then, it is now through God's grace. When we invite Jesus into our lives, we are filled with the Holy Spirit. It is through the Holy Spirit that we can hear God's voice and know how Jesus is leading us in our walk with Him. How awesome it is that everyone who is filled with the Holy Spirit can hear God's voice. God speaks through us. We are His messengers through the Holy Spirit who lives in us.

First Corinthians 14:1-5, "Pursue love, and desire spiritual gifts, but especially that you may prophesy. For he who speaks in a tongue does not speak to men but to God, for no one understands him; however, in the spirit he speaks mysteries. But he who prophesies speaks edification and exhortation and comfort to men. He who speaks in a tongue edifies himself, but he who prophesies edifies the church. I wish you all would speak with tongues, but even more that you prophesied; for he who prophesies is greater than he who speaks with tongues, unless indeed he interprets, that the church may receive edification."

A Short Study on the Prophetic

First Corinthians 12:31, "But earnestly desire the best gifts. And yet I show you a more excellent way"

It is plain to see in this Scripture that God wants to be heard clearly and distinctly to build up His church and to use His people to do so. If Father God says to desire the gifts, then when you desire you will receive.

On the day of Pentecost this promise was made available to us as God's children in Jesus Christ. (Acts 2:1–21)

New Testament Prophets are under the authority of the church. They are given one of the spiritual gifts explained in First Corinthians 12:1–10.

First Corinthians 14:29 "Let two or three prophets speak, and let the others judge."

New Testament prophetic words are tested through Scripture.

Ephesians 4:11–13 states, "He himself gave some to be apostles, some prophets, some evangelists, and some pastors and teachers, for the equipping of the saints for the work of ministry, for the edifying of the body of Christ, till we all come to the unity of the faith in the knowledge of the son of God to a perfect man, to the measure of the stature of the fullness of Christ."

First Corinthians 14:1 states, "Pursue love, and desire spiritual gifts, but especially that you may prophecy."

Paul encourages all to eagerly desire spiritual gifts, especially the gift of prophecy.

First Corinthians14:3 states, "But he who prophesies speaks edification and exhortation and comfort to men."

A prophetic word contains the working of the gift of wisdom and the gift of knowledge. The word of knowledge is a supernatural revelation concerning the present or the past. The word of wisdom looks to the future, which is the plan and purpose of God. The discerning of spirits and the gift of healing will also work, along with wisdom and knowledge many times in prophetic ministry.

As children of God we all are encouraged in Scripture to pursue the gift of prophecy but not all have the office of prophet.

Prophetic Word
Prophets and the Gift of Prophecy

There is a calling that is given to the one who performs the duty of prophet. This calling is placed on one who goes forth while pursuing the Word of God. A prophet functions within the church as a respected child of God and is someone who will not influence the body of Christ with their own judgment. A prophet who prophecies from his or her intellect will be judged, and this may have eternal consequences. To allow such a demonstration, there will be notification to all My church, and the one who is called to this office will be subject to the church under its jurisdiction. To be called as a prophet is to be duty-bound in the unity of the church to enrich its growth and spiritual enlightenment.

To speak the language of the Spirit in the gift of prophecy is entitling the one speaking to give what is rightfully theirs among the gifts. Is one gift more important than the others in the church? Will one receive more

> *than the other in the acknowledgment of the Father? Remember the unity of the body in My Word and know that I hold My children dear to Me in all that I give. It is of a clear day that My children see Me when they understand I love them no matter what their response is to My call, but the one who will answer My desire will indeed be blessed by the acknowledgment they will receive in their spirit. Blessed are they who know the commands of the Lord.*

Prophetic Words
God's Wisdom in Scripture

Hebrews 8:8–10 states, "Behold, the days are coming, says the Lord, when I will make a new covenant with the house of Israel and with the house of Judah not according to the covenant that I made with the fathers in the day when I took them by the hand to lead them out of the land of Egypt; because they did not continue in My covenant, and I disregarded them," says the Lord. 'For this is the new covenant I will make with the house of Israel after those days, says the Lord; I will put My laws in their mind and write them on their hearts; and I will be their God, and they shall be My people.'

The staying grace that comes to My washed children in Christ is a grace that will not falter. It rests on the attitude that is of My Spirit and will not bend for any evil spirit that tries to break the bond between Father and child. How I love to gather thee to My heart to hear My words in true prophecy. You are My loving children who have My laws written on your hearts. Worldly nonsense cannot compete with My power, so do not think that I would join with a heart that is straying to the wrong kingdom. The judgment in My Words comes through My Spirit, and My Spirit is connected to the body of Christ. Jesus stands as the head to judge in His church; as My people worship and adore Him, He will lead you in His righteousness and not lead you astray.

Psalm 7:7–8 says, "So the congregation of the peoples shall surround You; for their sakes, therefore, return on high. The Lord shall judge the peoples; judge me, O

Lord, according to my righteousness, and according to my integrity within me."

> *Hearing this prayer allows Me to be justified in making your way in Me a straight way according to My purpose in your life. Will you ask Me to judge you according to your righteousness? Will you come to Me and allow Me to make My way in you for My good purpose? It is only right and fitting that you are to hear My voice and read it to the people in the body of Christ. If you do not trust the voice of the Spirit that lives within you, who can you trust? Do not miss My voice that I wish to speak through you by not being attentive. I wish only to convey My will in My people, for through this they will remember that I am the judge of My people.*

Chapter 4

RECEIVING THE GIFT OF PROPHECY AND USING IT

*F*irst Corinthians 12:1–11 tells us about the spiritual gifts.

First Corinthians 12:7-11 states, "But the manifestation of the Spirit is given to each one for the profit of all: for to one is given the word of wisdom through the Spirit, to another the word of knowledge through the same Spirit, to another faith by the same Spirit, to another the word of knowledge through the same Spirit, to another faith by the same Spirit, to another gifts of healings by the same Spirit, to another the working of miracles, to another prophecy, to another discerning of spirits, to another different kinds of tongues, to another the interpretation of tongues. But one and the same

Spirit works all these things, distributing to each one individually as He wills."

First Corinthians 14:5 says, "I wish you all spoke with tongues, but even more that you prophesy; for he who prophesies is greater than he who speaks with tongues, unless indeed he interprets, that the church may receive edification."

Receive the Gift of Prophecy

First Corinthians 14:1 says, "Pursue love, and desire spiritual gifts, but especially that you may prophesy."

As we are willing to be used as God's instrument Holy Spirit will use us in our obedience to speak God's words from His heart. It should be stressed here that prophecy is divinely inspired and an anointed utterance. It is entirely supernatural. Prophecy is a manifestation of the Spirit of God.

Second Peter 1:20-21 says, "knowing this first, that no prophecy of Scripture is of any private interpretation, for prophecy never came by the will of man, but holy men of God spoke as they were moved by the Holy Spirit."

Review: How to receive the gift of prophecy

1. Desire the gift of prophecy.
2. Pray with others who have the gift.
3. Be submissive to the Holy Spirit.
4. Wait for the inspiration of the Holy Spirit.
5. Having faith and patience, you will receive.

Stirring Up the Gift of Prophecy

A foundation is needed in Scripture to flow in the gift of prophecy. A willingness to be available at any time to hear the Holy Spirit is essential. Being firmly planted in Christ will bring forth the desire to serve Him, which in turn is being obedient to His Word and being holy as He is holy. This will bring obedience to the Spirit of God and help you to keep your eyes on Him.

Acts 17:11 "These were more fair minded than those in Thessalonica, in that they received the word with all readiness, and searched the Scriptures daily to find out whether these things were so."

When speaking prophecy, total surrender and maintaining a close union with Christ and His word is most essential because God judges your intention.

Hebrews 10:19-24 "Therefore, brethren, having boldness to enter the holiest by the blood of Jesus, by a new and living way which He consecrated for us, through the veil, that is, His flesh, and having a High Priest over the house of God, let us draw near with a true heart in full assurance of faith, having our hearts sprinkled from an evil conscience and our bodies washed with pure water. Let us hold fast the confession of our hope without wavering, for He Who promised is faithful. And let us consider one another in order to stir up love and good works."

Blessing our brothers and sisters with God's love comes through the prophetic words we speak.

Prophetic Word

To want is to receive and then to receive is to speak in order for all to give God the glory. To mention the need in the church today would be to emphasize the scriptural values for all to pursue. In My gifts, there is the promise to perform to the best of My Spirit, and the will to preserve the holiness of God. What will My children lack for not hearing My word spoken in prophecy? It is pleasing in My sight for My children to have the desire to give to the church all I am willing to give for the pursuit of the righteousness of Christ.

I ask you not to be indulgent to seek just one gift but to seek the many I give in My will and My way for the Word to be mighty in power. Lend Me your ear today, and do not forget that I wait to be united with you in your prayer closet as your Intercessor stands always in your shadow to make the most of our time together.

Hearing God's Voice for Yourself

Acts 2:1–4 states, "When the day of Pentecost had fully come, they were all with one accord in one place.

And suddenly there came a sound from heaven, as of a rushing mighty wind, and it filled the whole house where they were sitting. Then there appeared to them divided tongues, as of fire, and one sat upon each of them. And they were all filled with the Holy Spirit and began to speak with other tongues, as the Spirit gave them utterance."

As children of God under the New Covenant, filled with the Holy Spirit, we are used as God's witnesses. Jesus said, before he was taken up in a cloud to heaven in Acts 1:8, "But you shall receive power when the Holy Spirit has come upon you; and you shall be witnesses to Me in Jerusalem, and in all Judea and Samaria, and to the end of the earth." Jesus has called us to be His messengers. When we are open to receive the gifts God has given to us, the Spirit of God gives us the power and will lead us forth!

John 10:4–5 states, "And when he brings out his own sheep, he goes before them; and the sheep follow him, for they know his voice. Yet they will by no means follow a stranger, but will flee from him, for they do not know the voice of strangers."

Galatians 4:6–7 states, "And because you are sons, God has sent forth the Spirit of His Son into your hearts, crying out, Abba, Father! Therefore you are no longer a slave but a son, and if a son, then an heir of God through Christ."

These Scriptures confirm that as sons and daughters of God, we will know His voice.

First John 3:1a says, "Behold what manner of love the Father has bestowed on us, that we should be called children of God!"

God loves us; we are His children. Therefore, we should expect to hear our Father God speak to us. To hear Him, we must have a relationship with Him, and that requires living the Christ-like life He has called us to live in Him.

First John 4:2–3a says, "By this you know the Spirit of God: Every spirit that confesses that Jesus Christ has come in the flesh is of God, and every spirit that does not confess that Jesus Christ has come in the flesh is not of God."

To test prophecy, there should first be a judgment made to confirm that the message conforms to Scripture. Any word which contradicts Scripture is false. Since God's Spirit lives within us, we will know it is our Lord's voice. When we place Jesus before all else based on the Scriptures, the doubts will lessen as we listen for God's voice.

Remember, One John 4:1 instructs us to "test the spirits to see whether they are from God." We do that by comparing the word to Scripture. Weigh what you are hearing: is it scriptural, is it appropriate, and does it make sense? We must remember the Holy Spirit gives us discernment. He is our filter, and He speaks to us from God's heart. The Holy Spirit wants us to be comfortable with what we are hearing.

"Pursue love, and desire spiritual gifts, but rather that you may prophesy." (First Corinthians 12:1)

One Corinthians 14:3 "But he who prophesies speaks edification and exhortation and comfort to men."

Prophecy is divinely inspired and an anointed utterance. It is entirely supernatural. Prophecy is a manifestation of the Spirit of God.

Second Peter: 1:17–21 states: "For He received from God the Father honor and glory when such a voice came to Him from the Excellent Glory: "This is My beloved Son, in whom I am well pleased." And we heard this voice which came from heaven when we were with Him on the holy mountain. And so we have the prophetic word confirmed, which you do well to heed as a light that shines in a dark place, until the day dawns and the morning star rises in your hearts; knowing this first, that no prophecy of Scripture is of any private interpretation, for prophecy never came by the will of man, but holy men of God spoke as they were moved by the Holy Spirit."

God wants to prophetically communicate to us, whether He is using His Word, speaking to His children personally, or through the prophetic gift of a believer.

Tips for prophesying:

1. Build up your mind in Scripture.
2. Come boldly to the throne of God in prayer. (Hebrews 4:16)
3. Focus in the spirit, don't let your mind wander, and keep your eyes on Jesus.
4. Relax in the spirit; don't try to think of words. You will know when Holy Spirit speaks to you.
5. Don't be intimidated by those around you. God knows your heart, and He will be your guide.

It takes practice. As it is in the natural to accomplish perfection, it also takes practice to raise your confidence that it is God's voice you are hearing.

GOD DESIRES TO SPEAK TO US TO GIVE US: GUIDANCE

Psalm 25:9–10 says, "The humble He guides in justice, and the humble He teaches His way. All the paths of the Lord are mercy and truth, to such as keep His covenant and His testimonies." When we need guidance, we must hear from God. He will always talk to us even if it is not a definite answer but will impart in us His peace and encouragement that will cause us to trust Him.

James 1:5–6 says: "If any of you lacks wisdom let him ask of God, who gives to all liberally and without reproach, and it will be given to him. But let him ask in faith, with no doubting for he who a doubt is like a wave of the sea driven and tossed by the wind. But let him ask in faith with no doubting, for he who doubts is like a wave of the sea and driven and tossed by the wind."

This scripture speaks about making decisions and hearing directions but also refers to hearing God's voice on a daily basis! God will answer us in His way, but not always in the way we are expecting!

ASSURANCE

First Peter 1:4 tells us that we "have an inheritance that is incorruptible, undefiled, and does not fade away that is reserved in heaven for us."

We hear God's voice in our spirit throughout each day even though we may not be aware of it. As we hear God's direction, we hear our destiny. We are not subject to the world's convictions of doing it man's way, but we are free in Jesus Christ to do it God's way. He desires us to hear Him in a more detailed way, to be confident that He is constantly with us, and to be sensitive to His presence. God wants to guide us in everything we do, for what concerns us, concerns Him.

It delights God's heart that we, His children, want to know Him and hear what He has to say to us on a personal level. In Christ Jesus, we have this privilege,

His favor, to know Him and acknowledge His love for us. How very blessed we are.

I would like you to ponder in the Spirit how much God loves you and how He has a purpose and a plan for you. You can have as much of God in Jesus Christ as you desire, and He will impart the measure He wants to give to you. He is the giver, and you who desires to know Him more, to honor Him, and give Him all of the glory, are His child.

Second Timothy 3:16-17 states, "All scripture is given by inspiration of God, and is profitable for doctrine, for reproof, for correction, for instruction in righteousness, that the man of God may be complete, thoroughly equipped for every good work."

God speaks to us through Scripture. His words are His promises to us. As He leads you in Scripture, speak it out as His promise to you; this is God's voice as He speaks to you through Scripture.

Deuteronomy 18:22 says, "when a prophet speaks in the name of the Lord, if the thing does not happen or come to pass, that is the thing which the Lord has not spoken; the prophet has spoken it presumptuously; you shall not be afraid of him. "

Remember that prophecy is given to the body of Christ for edification, exhortation and comfort. (First Corinthians 14:3)

The gift of prophecy means speaking out what you believe the Spirit is prodding you to speak and letting the church be the judge.

First Corinthians 12:10 tells us, "to another the interpretation of tongues." At times, words of prophecy will be spoken in other tongues, and an interpretation will be given. The interpreter is under the anointing of God and divinely speaks the word of prophecy as given through the Spirit of God. Although the interpreter does not know what was spoken in tongues in his own senses, it is through the Holy Spirit that it is revealed through him. Confirmation in Scripture is found in **First** Corinthians 12:6, 11

Prophetic Word

My Spirit will perform a good work in you, My children, who hunger for further knowledge to hear My voice. I will not hesitate giving you all that you require to go forth in My Word, but you must be willing to show yourselves as responsible children and go forth in and through My Spirit. While putting your trust in Me, My touch will be present for those who want My anointing to go forth in the church. My Word is free for the asking, but there is one cost and that would be the giving of yourself to be used as My instrument. Be still in your spirit and know I want to impart to you the nature of your Father, which is My will in your life.

HEARING THE VOICE OF GOD

Your spirit will be ready to receive what God wants to share with you as you sit in His presence. There is a chain reaction as we desire to hear God's voice. The Holy Spirit hears God speak to Him, the Holy Spirit speaks to your spirit, and then your spirit transmits it to your mind. What you are hearing in your mind is transcribed in writing or speaking. It all comes through your spirit-man where the Holy Spirit lives in you, in Christ Jesus who lives and moves and has His being within you. (Acts 17:28)

Jesus spoke to His disciples in John 16:12–15, saying:

"I still have many things to say to you, but you cannot bear them now. However, when He, the Spirit of Truth, has come, He will guide you into all Truth; for He will not speak on His own authority but whatever He hears He will speak, and He will tell you of things to come. He will glorify Me, for He will take of what is Mine and declare it to you. All things that the Father has are Mine. Therefore I said that He will take of Mine and declare it to you."

As we talk to God in prayer, we relate to Him what is on our heart: our cares, worries, concerns, and frustrations. He also wants to communicate to us what is on His heart. A relationship requires a two-way conversation; that is how two people get to know one another. As you have the opportunity to journal what you are hearing through God's Word in the Bible, or in your spirit-man through the Holy Spirit, God wants you to know He is with you and will speak to you in the way He knows you will be able to receive.

You may think of a Scripture, just a few words of a sentence, or get a picture in your mind. Whatever you are sensing, write it down. It only takes a step of faith, and the flow will begin from the Holy Spirit. The Word of God is always our main source of hearing God speak to us. It is through the written Word of God that we learn of His character and who we are in Christ, our Lord and Redeemer. What we are hearing from God to us personally must line up with His Word in the Bible. This is why we must renew our minds in the Word of God, so confusion cannot enter our minds and bring doubt. The Holy Spirit is our filter. He is our source of guidance in and through Jesus Christ.

Prayer: Father God, I believe I can hear Your voice. I believe You want me to hear Your voice. I open my heart to hear You more clearly for Your glory to be seen in my life.

Prophetic Word

The true form of all things is in My hand. I give to those who are truly and earnestly seeking My wisdom and knowledge. If I give freely to My children who are so discerning My truth, will I not gladly enrich them with the heart of the Truth-giver? Will I not take enjoyment over My children who seek Me over the world? I am in the midst of My children, having full charge of them as they allow Me. Will it not be My gladness that fills the hearts of those who are living in My Spirit to the fullness of My giving?

These are days filled with distasteful fruits from those who are giving from their flesh. I am asking you, My children, to discern with My Holy Spirit what is of flesh and what is of My Spirit. Will you not consider what I have said to you in My Word that seeking My kingdom through My Spirit will bring you far more in the light of knowledge than searching with your flesh? I do not come to you to be a forgetful voice but to be an anointing that falls upon you to be a double portion that will reap much as you are a blessing to others.

To stand for Christ is to stand with only the embellishment of God and not the world's approval. To be a disciple of Christ today is like a tree laden with fruit, standing in the middle of a barren land that shuns the likes of this fruit because of a God that calls the world to holiness.

My children, do not allow your fruit to spoil for lack of use, for the results will only end in disappointment for you. I have chosen you to accomplish My plan. Each of you is called to a purpose. Your willingness to live in My Spirit calls you to a new identity for all to see. Living for your God is a duty that demands much obedience and sacrifice, but I ask not of you what I will not do for you.

There will be much to see through My Spirit these days as I have prophesied. See the fulfillment of My words and be a working part of My body. Feed on My Word and enjoy the fellowship of My Spirit. I have many rich days ahead for you. I am a God who loves, and what I enjoy most is to bless My children. There is happiness in My presence. Let My Spirit flow and meet with Me each day at My throne of holiness.

Being Led by the Spirit

Keeping your connection open with God will keep your spiritual discernment sharp. Opening your spirit to hear God's voice can only be done through the Holy Spirit. God truly wants us to open our spiritual ears, so He can pour His love and peace into our hearts. Picture this: God is sitting on His throne with Jesus sitting at His right hand, and He is waiting to hear the voices of His children. As He hears us one by one, He responds and speaks into our spirits with words of love in His still, small voice, and we are filled with comfort and peace.

Hebrews 4:16
Let us therefore come boldly to the throne of grace that we may obtain mercy and find grace to help in time of need.

Conversations with God
What Does Scripture Say?

Now that we know we can hear God speak to us, we need to have confirmation from Scripture that tells us why we can and should hear God's voice. These are some of the Scriptures that tell us we are entitled to hear from God because we are now His children through Jesus Christ His only begotten Son:

First Corinthians 12:3 says, "Therefore I make known to you that no one speaking by the Spirit of God calls Jesus accursed, and no one can say that Jesus is Lord except by the Holy Spirit." Jesus took authority over all things concerning our lives when we invited Him to be our Savior and Lord. He lives in us through the power of the Holy Spirit who will give us wisdom to discern the Spirit of God from other spirits.

John 10:3–5 states, "To him the door keeper opens, and the sheep hear his voice; and he calls his own sheep by name and leads them out. And when he brings out his own sheep, he goes before them; and the sheep follow him, for they know his voice. Yet they will by no means follow a stranger, but will flee from him for they do not know the voice of strangers."

We know the voices of those who live close to us; therefore, we will know the voice of the one who died for us and will lead us in His righteousness.

Psalm 23:1–2 states, "The Lord is my shepherd; I shall not want. He makes me to lie down in green pastures; He leads me beside the still waters."

Galatians 4:6–7 states, "And because you are sons, God has sent forth the Spirit of His Son into your hearts, crying out, Abba, Father! Therefore you are no longer a slave but a son, and if a son, then an heir of God through Christ."

Because we are sons of God, He is now our Father who wants to give us individual encouragement and directions for the plans and purposes He has for our lives.

Jeremiah 29:11 says, "For I know the thoughts that I think toward you," says the Lord, "thoughts of peace and not of evil to give you a future and a hope."

If He is our Father, we should expect to hear His wisdom. God wants to fill us with His peace as we hear Him speak to us through His Word or in any way that He knows is best.

First John 3:1 says, "Behold what manner of love the Father has bestowed on us, that we should be called children of God."

To hear God we need a relationship with Him. When I first started to hear God's voice, I would question if it was God's voice, my voice, or the voice of Satan. I would rebuke the spirit of fear and ask the Holy Spirit to come. I knew the Holy Spirit had me in training to hear God's voice. I would wait until I knew I had the peace of Jesus before writing what I was hearing. It is the Holy Spirit in us that gives us that peace.

Isaiah 55:9–11 states, "For as the heavens are higher than the earth so are My ways higher than your ways, and My thoughts than your thoughts. For as the rain comes down, and the snow from heaven, and do not return there, but water the earth, and make it bring forth and bud, that it may give seed to the sower and bread to the eater, so shall My word be that goes forth from My mouth; it shall not return to Me void, but it shall accomplish what I please, and it shall prosper in the thing for which I sent it."

Hearing God's voice is natural for all who are walking in the Spirit and not the flesh! God's children want to hear God's direction; they are hungry to hear more, to have His guidance to fulfill their purpose and destiny for their lives!

Testimonies after Receiving a Prophetic Word

This is a testimony from Mike W., in Pennsylvania

After my divorce, I moved to another state to be closer to my sister and brother who were seriously ill. I did not make the move in time to see my sister before she died, and my brother was back in the hospital. I was in an emotional turmoil.

I attended a house church meeting with a friend and received a prophetic word from a prophet. The words I heard from God, as the Holy Spirit spoke directly to my heart, were words of encouragement. Where I was rejected, I am now accepted; my family will be my sisters and brothers in Christ. He spoke joy and restoration over me. God said His anointing will not be held back, but I will go forth with joy. I could feel the love of God as He said He would be with me every step of the way. God knew about my life and cared enough to let me know that He is fully involved in the next steps of my destiny. This was the springboard I needed to continue to not only walk forward but to have times of soaring in the spirit as well.

Rabon J. in Maryland, received direction and encouragement after receiving a prophetic word

I received a word of prophecy at a time I was praying how I was to go forth in ministering to people through the anointing of the Holy Spirit for healing. The prophetic words I heard told me how I would go forward with boldness to many people and be an example of how God healed me miraculously. I would be a testimony of the healing blood of Jesus Christ. God said He would put a pen in my hand, and I would write about the testimonies of the healings I have seen. This prophetic word proceeded to tell me I had angels who would be with me to help me. I received encouragement of how God had made me ready to be an example of His love. Since this prophecy, the Lord has sent me to pray for more than 1,000 people at various churches, outreach events, and on the streets. A high percentage of those people were miraculously healed! The prophecy I received was very encouraging at that particular time. I received direction, and since then everything that was said has come to pass. I am now writing a book that the Holy Spirit has prompted me to write about my experiences.

Chapter 5
JUDGING PROPHECY

To test a message of prophecy, ask yourself:

1. Is the content of the message in line with Christian teaching?
2. The message must confirm with basic Christian teaching.
3. Anything that contradicts Scripture is false.
4. Weigh the prophetic words you are hearing and be aware of confirmation in your spirit.
5. If you have any doubts what you are hearing is from the Holy Spirit share with someone who is mature in the gift of the prophetic for affirmation.

How does your spirit respond? Do you feel peaceful, confused, or fearful? Test the spirits to see if it is true prophecy. There are times when you will not feel any response. This is normal and does not necessarily mean you are not hearing words from the Holy Spirit. There will be a peace in your spirit as God speaks to you through words that are loving, comforting, and encouraging. The Holy Spirit filters the words you are hearing from Father God's heart. He will confirm if the words you are hearing in your spirit are from the Father.

* When God speaks correction, He is beckoning us to repent, to walk in His ways, and to go from glory to glory.
* Beware of anyone who always prophesies in a negative way. This is an indication they are prophesying their own opinions.
* Does the prophecy glorify Jesus Christ?

A true word from the Lord will bring forth good fruit. Most of the prophecies we hear are not predictions but will give new life, peace, hope, and love to those who are hearing it in the Spirit. A word that is not from the Lord will produce bad fruit: strife, anger, jealousy, judgment, and so forth.

Testing prophecies will come with maturity as we listen and open our hearts with a discerning spirit. As the congregation hears a prophetic word, many times there are others who are hearing the same message from the Holy Spirit, but not in the exact wording. When this happens, it is helpful to give confirmation not only to the one who spoke the word but to the people who are among those who heard the word. This is helpful to those who are growing in the gift of prophecy.

Prophetic Words
God's Wisdom in Scripture

Deuteronomy 18:22 , "When a prophet speaks in the name of the Lord, if the thing does not happen or come to pass, that is the thing which the Lord has not spoken; the prophet has spoken it presumptuously; you shall not be afraid of him."

> *This message is clear. It proclaims the deity of the Lord Almighty and acknowledges the sinfulness of man. This also warns of how man does not always hear in the right spirit. But I will prevail, and My authority will reign in the end, so be not afraid of what man says, but hear My Words in your own heart and put fear in its proper place.*

Titus 1:15–16 , "To the pure all things are pure, but to those who are defiled and unbelieving nothing is pure; but even their mind and conscience are defiled. They profess to know God but in works they deny him, being abominable, disobedient, and disqualified for every good work."

Looking at the field ready for harvest, I see the crippled not only in body but in spirit. It is for a while that the world sees those who are torn and lends a helping hand, but when the time becomes a burden for them in good works, they get weary and turn away. How will a world be rid of the enemy's deceit if those who know Me do not reach out in the love of Christ? If only for the time you have left in living the life as a disciple you reach out to those who are, in fact, corrupted by the world, the change would be recognized in the Spirit. One person matters in such a sin-filled world?-.

Times have not changed, My dear ones, for the expectancy is still here in My heart to see My children, who are growing in the

Spirit, reach out and make a difference in a world that does not see a living God. In your pursuit to go forward in the ministry of My choice, astounding differences can be made to turn corruption into purity. It is your choice to be in full discipleship or to tarry and never have the full peace of one who is serving God with all of your heart.

First Corinthians 14:3 , "But he who prophesies speaks edification and exhortation and comfort to men."

Hear the Words I send through My prophets with your spirit and not your mind. Hold onto those words for they are dear and counted as they enter the hearts of My children. Lend not your ears to the so-called fantasies that lead to disappointment, but give your whole being to the proposal that comes from the throne of God. That is, take what is said, weigh it, try it, and know that to partake of it is a good thing.

First Corinthians 12:10 , "to another the working of miracles, to another prophecy, to another discerning of spirits, to another different kinds of tongues, to another the interpretation of tongues."

What makes a definite difference in the making of a Spirit-filled Christian? Is it justified to say the Father of His children would not give a discerning way? Do I give to add to My importance in the sight of man, or do I allow the Spirit to work in proportion to one's faith? How do I, your Father, choose to whom I shall give My power? You will not fail to recognize the truth and the answer to these questions, for this has been given to you from My Spirit. Know that I assure My children in the best of My ways; also know that I will give in proportion to My will and hope you will receive with your faith to proclaim the gospel of Jesus Christ to the world.

First Thessalonians 2:8–9, "So affectionately longing for you, we were well pleased to impart to you not only the gospel of God, but also our own lives, because you had become dear to us. For you remember, brethren, our labor and toil; for laboring night and day, that we might not be a burden to any of you, we preached to you the gospel of God.

> During ministry, there should be a definite focus on the needs of others and not your own. In a church that has taken on the responsibility of preaching God's Word, there should not be a lack of ministering among one another. When going outside the church to minister to the world, your trials should not be shared with those to whom you are ministering. In a qualified ministry, there should be the wisdom of the Spirit and not the pleasure of self to add counsel. In a world filled with the wisdom of self, I ask you, My children, to seek the wisdom of your God. In a delighted way I want you to accept what My Spirit gives to you.

> In a relationship between Father and child, there can be a delay to welcome the call of the Spirit, which can cause a negative reaction in the flesh. Would the call to be a surrendered disciple be so tiring that Jesus would not refresh the spirit in the one who

is so pleasing to their Father? Enjoying the work of your Lord is giving all of yourself without burdening others with your trials.

Chapter 6

YOU ARE GOD'S MOUTHPIECE

Hearing the Word of God for Others

Many years ago, when I was a new Christian and first began to hear God speak through me to others, I would write it. I did not have the boldness to speak it, and honestly, I knew very little about prophecy. I only knew that it was God I was hearing. I had much to learn. Praise God the Holy Spirit was drawing me to keep my eyes on Jesus and not the gift.

Speaking a Prophetic Word

You may feel or sense a pounding of your heart or shaking in your body. I had this when I first started to speak prophecy corporately. I had such a pounding in my heart I knew I had to release what I was hearing from the Holy Spirit. I stepped out in faith, opened my mouth in obedience and surrendered to the Spirit's leading.

What you are sensing can be a thought, a word, a sentence, or a picture. Sometimes you will know the essence of the message, but generally you will only get a few words. It is then you must trust that the Holy Spirit will speak the full message He wants to give. Just as you knew the Holy Spirit gave you the beginning of the message, you will know when He has finished. This is all done through faith by surrendering to the Him.

If you miss the opportunity to speak what you feel the Holy Spirit wants to give because you are not sure or lack the boldness, do not feel condemnation. You are building your confidence. God knows your heart and that your desire is to do His will. Remember, God loves us for who we are, His beloveds, and does not love us because of our performance.

The word of the Lord may come as a peace and tranquility or as an excited power that surges forth like a bubbling up in your spirit.

Prophecy may be a song, a prayer, or praises to God

One Peter 4:10-11, As each one has received a gift, minister it to one another, as good stewards of the manifold grace of God. If anyone speaks let him speak as the oracles of God. If anyone ministers, let him do it as with the ability which God supplies, that in all things God may be glorified through Jesus Christ, to whom belong the glory and the dominion forever and ever. Amen.

When giving a word to an individual, it is good protocol to approach them and ask permission to give the word you feel you have received.

What Prophecy Is and What It Imparts in Our Lives

"The testimony of Jesus is the spirit of prophecy." (Revelation 19:10) Prophecy is revealing the heart of God in and through His Son Jesus Christ, speaking forth the mind of God under the inspiration of the Holy Spirit. It is the outflow of the heart and nature of God.

Prophetic ministry reveals God's truth and erases the lies of the enemy. Prophecy opens our hearts as God's very breath breaks unbelief and refreshes the life of Jesus Christ in us to edify, exhort, and comfort. (One Corinthians 14:3) When God speaks, the old nature in us cannot override the new creature in Christ that now resides in us. The old is gone, and the new is there to stay as we keep our eyes on Jesus.

Prophecy manifests God's supernatural power that is a witness to who He is. Prophecy ministers life to the one receiving the word, which is God's love to His beloved. This helps us to know God cares for the now in our lives, as well as the future. Prophecy usually confirms what God is already speaking to us. True prophecy is always positive and spoken with love. Psalm 85:8 says, "I will hear what the Lord will speak for he will speak peace to his people and his saints."

Prophecy must always line up with the Word of God. It is never spoken through our own intellect but always as we are hearing the Holy Spirit. Prophecy encourages us to pursue God for fresh revelation from the Holy Spirit, to come closer to God's heart, and to have an intimate relationship with Him. Prophecy is conditional; hearing God's voice requires stepping out in obedience in order to bring forth its revelation. If you are sensing the Holy Spirit has a prophetic word for you to speak, it is up to you to step out in faith and be obedient. God will not impose His will on us but expects us to surrender our will to Him for His glory.

Prophecy shows us how to pray. God can bring forth a word to the body of Christ, or to an individual, to pray and intercede about a situation. Prophecy brings healing. Hearing a direct word from God spoken to the corporate body or an individual can bring healing. As we hear God speak to us directly concerning our situations, it confirms that God knows what is happening in our lives. This brings peace and confirmation to our spirit that God knows what is on our hearts and He is working it out. This deepens our relationship with God and enriches our faith to believe and trust Him.

Prophecy can be a warning. A word from God, delivered in love, can call us to repentance and into a closer walk with God our Father. Example: I once gave a word to my church that was calling us to release all we are holding onto, things only He could change, and we could do nothing about. There was a great move of His Spirit as God went on to say, "to hold onto those things would bring a delay of His blessings in our lives."

Prophecy is always spoken with God's love, never in judgment or condemnation. Prophecy is God speaking His heart to His child for encouragement, comfort, and edification! His very breath goes into the spirit of the one receiving His word and will convey His truth.

John 16:13–15 says, "However, when He, the Spirit of Truth, has come, He will guide you into all truth; for He will not speak on His own authority, but whatever He hears He will speak; and He will tell you things to come. He will glorify Me, for He will take of what is Mine and declare it to you."

A Word from God always draws us closer to Him. Where Satan has lied God reveals His Truth through His Word therefore confusion is turned into Gods Truth!

Prophecy Is for Breakthrough

The one receiving the word will receive the revelation or interpretation. The one speaking God's word is only the messenger; once the word is given, it is released to the one receiving.

It takes time to train your spirit. Like an athlete trains his or her body, we must train our spirit to respond to God's Spirit, the Holy Spirit. You can train yourself to hear God's voice. You can and will know the difference between your voice and the voice of God.

Chapter 7
PROPHETIC INTERCESSION

The Holy Spirit Is Leading You to Pray

We can get a sense, a feeling, that we need to pray but do not know how to pray. This, I believe, is a call to pray, in your understanding or your prayer language. When we pray in the Spirit, we are praying as the Holy Spirit leads. This is prophetic prayer. Praying prophetically is praying God's will for specific prayer needs. The more sensitive we are to how the Holy Spirit is speaking to us, the easier it will be for us to respond to the obedience of His call.

First Corinthians 14:14–15 says, "For if I pray in a tongue my spirit prays, but my understanding is unfruitful. What is the conclusion then? I will pray with the spirit, and I will also pray with the understanding. I will sing with the spirit, and I will also sing with the understanding."

As we pray in the spirit, we are opening our hearts to hear how the Holy Spirit wants to pray through us. We will have a deeper understanding of how Father God wants to use us during our times of prayer. Just as we speak prophetically over individuals or corporately, we can speak prophetically through our prayers of intercession.

Years ago, when I led a weekly intercession group, I had the sense in my spirit there was more to what God wanted to do through our prayers. As I was praying one morning, I heard a definite word from the Lord about our weekly prayer meetings. The message went something like this: "As you gather in intercession with others, I would have you pray not with your own senses but wait on the Spirit and He will lead you and guide you in how to pray. Your prayers are availing nothing if you are praying the mind of man!" Of course, I was shaken by these words. I repented and asked for God's guidance. I shared the word with the others, and from that time on when we met for prayer, it was definitely led by the Holy Spirit !

God's beloveds, believe and know you hear God's voice! You hear His voice for yourself, for your sisters and brothers, and for all for whom you pray!

IT'S TIME TO SPEAK

There is a move of God for such a time as this that is calling for God's people to embrace the world with His love. God is calling His people to step into a time that He has called forth, a time when His extravagant love is bringing a harvest into His kingdom. He is calling us to know His voice, to speak His voice, and to be His ambassadors of love to a dying world. I want to encourage you to seek God like never before, and to desire more of Him as you have never done before. The Holy Spirit wants to speak through you, God's child, to seek first the kingdom and all these things will follow. If you want more of God, there is no way He will deny you, but we must remember He wants more of us.

Discover the wind of the Spirit, the breath of God in you. As God speaks, His breath in us goes into the atmosphere to change evil to good! What has taken years to cause harm, God, the Creator of all things, can change in a moment. He never creates havoc but always peace and harmony. He is the restorer of the breach. He rescues us from the pit and wants us to rely on Him through His Son Jesus Christ who lives in us. Jesus is the way, the door to God's heart. The prophetic is God's voice that goes forth to create newness of life. It is His goodness that speaks life to our spirit. He wants us to discover the power of the wind of His Spirit that lives in us.

Let us pray and ask the Holy Spirit for more, that He would lead us in the pursuit to discover the power within us, and for God's glory to manifest in the atmosphere. This will cause God's goodness to be revealed as we speak supernaturally through the Holy Spirit. Just think of all that is in the supernatural that has not been revealed to us! If we are hungry for more of God, He will reveal more to us if it is for His glory. He wants us to share what He is giving us to speak whenever and wherever we have the opportunity.

There is nothing God will not do in and through us; He wants to reveal Who He is to us. He is the Great I am and the Creator of all things. Jeremiah 33:3 says,

"Call to Me, and I will answer you, and show you great and mighty things, which you do not know."

Chapter 8
GOD'S WISDOM IN SCRIPTURE

As I was preparing a teaching on the prophetic, the Holy Spirit began to give me Scriptures and speak to me about God's wisdom that would enhance further knowledge to His people. I understood this was not an extension of His written Word but to bring a greater understanding.

Prophetic Words
God's Wisdom in Scripture

Psalm 105:1–4 states, "Oh, give thanks to the Lord! Call upon his name; make known His deeds among the peoples! Sing to Him, sing psalms to Him; talk of all His wondrous works! Glory in His holy Name; Let the hearts of those rejoice who seek the Lord! Seek the Lord and His strength; seek His face ever more!"

As I ask My children to go forth in the power of My Spirit, the fire of My Spirit will produce the excitement of a love relationship that is always alive and stable. In My covenant relationship with My children, the roots extend as far as My throne and in no way can these fruits be torn if your commitment to Me is true. Making a way for My glory to be seen will become the strength of all who seek Me with a clean heart. How will I be increasing My works in these days of such abominations aimed at Me in the world? Will it take the likes of the miracles of past days to show My power? I call you, My children, to a clearer commitment, one that gives Me glory and allows a Savior to lead you into all of My righteousness. Would I ask of you something that is impossible? Glory in Me, My children, for the very heart of Me lives in you, and I have resurrected you into the new life in My Son.

Matthew 17:20 says, "So Jesus said to them, 'Because of your unbelief; for assuredly, I say to you, if you have faith as a mustard seed, you will say to this mountain, move from here to there, and it will move; and nothing will be impossible for you.'"

The call to My church is to go forth in the faith that rests in the people. It is not a task that calls for My people to serve for the love of duty but to serve for the love of their God. One who chooses to join in a relationship with the Holy Trinity relinquishes all of their old life and starts afresh. There comes then, a new heart to replace that which was once filled with darkness. When trusting in faith, there is an absolute choice to give of one's entire being. To pronounce faith but not live it allows the old image of the world to be portrayed and not the new life in Christ Jesus. Emotions may play at the heart, but what is instilled in the heart through the Holy Spirit's power will wrench out all of the old nature. Lack of faith comes when one tries in their strength and not in the Spirit's giving. Therefore, be all that I wish you to be, willing servants who serve me well. I will do the indwelling with My Spirit, and the hands of Jesus will pull you up the mountains that need to be climbed.

John 12:17–18 says, "Therefore the people, who were with Him when He called Lazarus out of his tomb and raised him from the dead, bore witness. For this reason the people also met Him, because they heard that He had done this sign."

I have called you, My children, to My truth for all to see what your God can do. In all the hopes of the world, there never can be such hope as there is in Jesus. To follow the path in the journey He leads is to be in all wonder of His majesty. Have I called you to be quality children of My kingdom or to be lost in your faith when you reach out to those who are hurting? It would not be a testimony of your God's will if you were to give the advice the world would give. To see the glory of My kingdom is to give in the name of Jesus.

The world goes on wanting more and more power when all they need to believe is My kingdom come, My will be done on earth as it is in heaven. My good and true children want no power for themselves but to give it all to the good, for God to be praised. As I hold onto you, My children, I will allow no other to take My place, no matter how the offenses try to delay you in your walk. My glory is but a glimpse of what you have seen, and the fullness of it will be in the glory of the kingdom I hold for those who are fixed in My spiritual love.

Acts 24:16 says, "This being so, I myself always strive to have a conscience without offense toward God and men."

How can one serve a God that is righteous and good without first having the cleansing grace of a Savior? How can the world accept a God who knows all, tells all, and reaches out to those who are lost? Can one reach Me with an unclean heart? Can one feel the response from a God who loves and cares, no matter what the circumstance? There comes a most satisfying confidence through My Spirit when one who serves Christ not only feels satisfied in their soul, but also gives witness to this fact in the way they treat others. Will one who strives to be clean of heart and mind be unjust in serving others? Will they not be a stable servant of Christ if they practice holy living and holy trust? Make clear to all who see you, My children, that you are a child of God who hears your God well in all you do, for this is a good witness for those who need to hear Me and have their heart filled with Christ.

Psalm 17:6 says, "I have called upon You, for You will hear me, O God; incline Your ear to me, and hear my speech."

Transferring your thoughts into prayers should be done in a discerning way. You will find My Spirit will lead you in all you do and all you say. You must realize that trusting in all things that I send to you, as the result of your prayers, will bring you what you need for proper guidance in your life as you serve Me well. How many times have I shown My love without a prayer given? How many times have I sent to even the ones who do not acknowledge Me a love gift in many forms? To discern My love for you, My children, you must ask the Spirit for discernment for you to have what I would have you receive. When you come to Me with a cleansed and uplifted heart, you are established in spiritual righteousness and will receive My direction for your needs and desires. As you come to Me, asking with faith, I will give what I know is best for you. Now remember to store in your spirit the spiritual attitude of expectancy, for it will be in My justification and My timing that all things you have asked for will come to pass.

Psalm 25:14 says, "The secret of the Lord is with those who fear Him. And He will show them His covenant."

Trust in hearing My voice is likened to the joy of knowing Jesus, for knowing He is within you is true trust. Much is to be conveyed to My ones who are seeking Me in the Spirit. My heart is filled with joy when I hear My children crying out to Me, for it is the Spirit's work that has been accomplished in rending their hearts. Those who know Me will not be afraid to hear what I have to say, for it is in the peaceful heart of Jesus that true hearing is found. I wait to see those who are expecting because of their acknowledgment of the Word. To believe with all your heart and all your soul that I am God is to believe that your life must reflect My joy and not the displeasure of the world. Hold to My truth in My Word, and you will know what I say is real truth, for the truth of the world is unstable.

First John 3:2 says, "Beloved, now we are children of God; and it has not yet been revealed what we shall be, but we know that when He is revealed, we shall be like Him, for we shall see Him as He is."

To make known to My children the reality of the day they are living is to insure them of their rightful place in My kingdom. My Spirit manifests in each and every child of God to make known My presence in the way He chooses. In each of My children, there will appear that sense of My presence as I choose to make Myself known through My Spirit. To have direct contact with Christ is to know Him now and forever. Be aware of the true sacrifice that must be made in the gifts given, for they are given for the glory of God and not for the use of man at his own will.

Romans 8:16–18 says, "The Spirit Himself bears witness with our spirit that we are children of God, and if children, then heirs, heirs of God and joint heirs with Christ, if indeed we suffer with Him, that we may also be glorified together. For I consider the sufferings of this present time are not worthy to be compared with the Glory which shall be revealed in us."

Turning over a life to Christ is the difference between day and night. You were in darkness, but then the light of Christ brought you forth to see the glory of God. I want to bring forth the evidence of My love for what I have created. Why do those who spoil My glory behave in such a way as to disturb the focus of My dear ones who are in Christ? Those who are of the evil doers do not care for such things as the fear of God or the travails of an enemy that waits in every avenue of life. When one tells the tale of Christ and His resurrection, there is an outpouring of life-giving virtues through My glory. Having the hopes of a mission for Christ will bring confidence from spiritual knowledge and satisfaction to the one who needs uplifting in their spirit. This spiritual knowledge will also show others that a child of God is one who withstands all sufferings in the name of Jesus with a peaceful heart.

Luke 8:19–21 says, "Then His mother and brothers came to Him and could not approach Him because of the crowd. And it was told Him by some, who said, 'Your mother and Your brothers are standing outside, desiring to see You.' But He answered and said to them, 'My mother and My brothers are these who hear the word of God and do it.'"

Multiply the hearing of the Word with the sound of the Spirit, and you will gather more knowledge. To trust one another in the body is to hold to the virtues of a house in good order and will instill in those who are unsure of God's wisdom to come and seek in the Spirit. Hallowed is the way of those who are covered in My Spirit. They are taking the responsibility to not only go forth for the true God they chose but also acknowledge this in a way that is truly righteous in an unrighteous world. I must emphasize the importance of spiritual growth in the body of Christ, for it is growing in knowledge that enhances the growth of the church to show to the world. To reach the world in spiritual knowledge will be an undertaking that comes only in My Spirit. Do this in holiness, and My purpose will be fulfilled in all you do.

First Timothy 6:20-21 says, "O Timothy! Guard what was committed to your trust, avoiding the profane and idle babblings and contradictions of what is falsely called knowledge, by professing it some have strayed concerning the faith. Grace be with you. Amen"

How do I care for you, My beloveds, who are living in the world but are not of it? Does the rest of the world, who lives in darkness, not see how My children are guided by God's wisdom? I will accomplish all that I have set out to do and to care for those who are obedient in all I want to accomplish. The knowledge of the world waits lingering in the shadows. This is always how the enemy works even in My children who are sometimes not aware of the falsehoods that can appear in a shining light. When I entrust My children with what I have given, it is so they can show the glory of the kingdom of God and not for the glory of man, to be raised up higher for self-gratification. Remember the times when you were afraid the world's ways were entering into your life? I ask you to seek protection in prayer, asking for the wisdom I want to impart to you. Be aware of those who follow other gods in ways that proclaim signs and wonders that are not recognized in your spiritual discernment. Any who are among the dead in virtue are not entitled to My ways. I am responsible for My own, and their way will be cleared because I am God.

Matthew 14:27 says, "But immediately Jesus spoke to them saying, 'Be of good cheer! It is I; do not be afraid."

I am not like the world and its ways. I am not the partisan who takes part in any way that will cause My children to hear a word that would do them harm. Trust in those who are Mine, those who are in tune with the Spirit. This will make all come together for the good of those who walk as Jesus walked. To keep your eyes on good and not evil will help all who want to hear with the Spirit rather than the flesh. You are My children and have the mind of Christ. Do not fear the enemy who would like you to think you are hearing from him. Remember you have the mind of Christ because of your rebirth. Take that remembrance with you at all times, for I will always be ready to speak to you.

Romans 8:25 says, "But if we hope for what we do not see, we eagerly wait for it with perseverance."

Having patience in My timing is having the blessed assurance that is sent with the Spirit's knowledge. This is the glory that will be seen in My children who know My truth while others are impatient to wait and go forth without the Spirit's guide. Walking in faith will bring My wisdom. The time for true wisdom will not be late to come to My children if their hope is stable. They will receive My wisdom that cannot be compared to the wisdom of the world.

Psalm 117:10 says, "I believed; therefore I said, I am greatly afflicted."

Believing with great faith will cause those around you to be so astounded and may bring persecution. At these times, let the Cross be your strength. Abide in the knowledge of the Lord, and He will be with you. Do not be afraid of those who try to afflict you, for they will be confronted by My might, and you, My children, will be filled with My peace.

First Kings 12:8 says, "But he rejected the advice which the elders had given him, and consulted the young men who had grown up with him, who stood before him."

Wisdom and knowledge flow from My Spirit into My church. Why is it that My children do not trust the Body of Christ or those who are like-minded? Would I, your caretaker, do a distrustful thing to My people? What more would your Father give but His best for His children? In the church, I have provided a way to seek wisdom and knowledge for those who need the way to be made clearer. Trusting those in the body of Christ will bring forth more and more of My voice to be heard. It is My desire that My children never lack hearing My wisdom. Never assume that your God will not bring an answer but know that in My holiness I will give you guidance. As you ask in reverence, I will answer you, for I know your trust is in

Jesus. Come together in the Spirit as one and seek Me through the Body of Christ because they are My voice.

John 14:7, says, "If you had known Me, you would have known My Father also; and from now on you know Him and have seen Him."

John 14:12-14, "Most assuredly I say to you, he who believes in Me, the works that I do he will do also; and greater works than these he will do, because I go to My Father. And whatever you ask in My name, that I will do, that the Father may be glorified in the Son. If you ask anything in My name I will do it."

My promise is made clear in My Word. I make a way for My Spirit to speak in many ways to My children. When you hope to hear your Father's direction, I will bring the endearment we have together as a bond that will never break. Hear me in the full truth I wish to give; know that in Jesus Christ all things are possible because the impossible was washed away by His blood. Why would a God who loves justice not speak to His children to guide, nurture, and fill them with the joy of the Spirit? Hear me, all My children, for I am your Father who desires our relationship to deepen through My Spirit.

Revelation 1:8 says, "I am the Alpha and the Omega, the Beginning and the End," says the Lord, "who is and who was and who is to come, the Almighty."

These words are to be held in the highest value. Sadly, the world looks to Me as one who holds the world loosely in His hands. How I long to make known the real and true feelings of My heart to those who are making a mockery of My power. Promises are seen in My Word and should be received for full value. The days are here when much of the heartaches of the lost will be seen. As they continue to walk in the flesh, they will go deeper and deeper in desperation. Admitting defeat and surrendering to a God who loves them and cares could be their newfound hope, but instead they try harder and harder to escape by running into the enemy's hands. You, My ones, are holding the key to their very lives, the key being your Savior, Jesus

Christ. To unlock the days of darkness and allow the light of Christ to shine, there must be a willingness to share that which He has gladly given to you, and that is your freedom from the clutches of him who hides in the darkness, Satan. Let the fire of My Spirit burn more brightly in you today, My precious ones, for it will light the way for those who are looking for the path to My kingdom.

Malachi 3:1 says, "Behold, I send My messenger, and he will prepare the way before Me. And the Lord, whom you seek, will suddenly come to His temple, even the Messenger of the covenant, in whom you delight. Behold, He is coming, says the Lord of hosts."

Being washed and purified in these days of preparation for the coming of Christ will be enhanced as My children hear My voice. I speak through My children for a purpose and not for their satisfaction. If there were no words to hear from the throne, would there not be a dryness that would be felt in the church today? Where does the power come from that fills the church? It comes from the Holy Spirit. Will you, My children, not hear My cry for a clearer vision for the church today? Will you not hear the word of the messenger sent long ago? That message was "Prepare ye the way of the Lord." Hear the cry of the Spirit of God, for as the way was prepared for Christ's coming, it must also be prepared for His coming again.

Deuteronomy 4:12 says, "And the Lord spoke to you out of the midst of the fire. You heard the sound of the words, but saw no form; you only heard a voice."

Which Commandments are close to your heart? Are they not the words spoken that day to My people? I wish to melt the hearts of My children today with the fire of the Spirit that will become the desires of your Father. I will bring the coolness of the living waters of Christ who stands beside you, ready to make your way easy as He guides you in His righteousness. I am the beginning and the end. What I was in the beginning, I am now. I wish to shower My children with the grace that will always be from My heart. Let the people hear the voice of their Father. Do not hold back the fire of the Spirit, for the way of the Lord will hold true to Scripture, and they who hear will be encouraged to follow My way.

Acts 4:4 says, "However, many of those who heard the word believed; and the number of the men came to be about 5,000."

"Come to hear the words of the Lord" should be the message of all the church. To be touched by the Spirit means there must be a commitment from My people to show the working of the Spirit among them. Will this not bring many to be washed in the blood of Christ? Hearing words from the throne will not only lift up the body of Christ but will touch those who do not believe in a living God. I make Myself known to all who are open to hear My voice. Will you make yourself available to the Spirit to speak to all who need to hear My voice? Filling your temple with the Spirit has called you to a greater commitment through the Spirit. I

ask you to be open to let Him work as He wills in you.

John 14:6–7 says, "Jesus said to him, 'I am the way, the truth, and the life. No one comes to the Father except through Me. If you had known me, you would have known My Father also; and from now on you know Him and have seen Him.'"

Making a way for My children is the pleasure of My heart. To know Me is to love Me, and to love Me is to add to the desires of your heart. Placing My Son above all else makes the way for My heart to flourish in My children. This is the only way. Speaking truth comes in a moment given through My grace as My Spirit moves in rapid speed to bring those who are in need to My kingdom. How is it that those who know me will not adhere to the openness that could be between us? Take this Scripture to heart and meditate on it. You know Me in the holiness of Christ. Speaking words through you is part of this foundation we have together. Hold to what is dear in the heavenly knowledge and not to the knowledge of the world that sways you away from a close relationship with your God.

Mark 11:12–14 says, "Now the next day, when they had come out from Bethany, He was hungry. And seeing from afar a fig tree having leaves, He went to see if perhaps He would find something on it. When He came to it, He found nothing but leaves, for it was not the season for figs. In response Jesus said to it, "let no one eat fruit from you ever again."

Being in full bloom for Christ is being able to have the fruit of the Spirit be picked in order that more fruit may be allowed to grow in larger quantity. While in season, the fruit of My children feeds the hungry to overflowing. The Spirit of God is always waiting to go forth to refresh those who need the zest of My Spirit to feed their hunger. Would I, your Father, not prune your life in order for it to bear the fruit I wish? Would I, your Father, not be gentle with nurturing you as I call you to be what I wish you to be? Do not allow your life in Christ to wither for lack of knowledge for I will fertilize you as you are growing. It is My responsibility to feed you and I will feed you well. Ask Me, and you will receive not only the gift of speaking My words but also the fruitfulness of the assurance that it is I who speaks. Take what you hear as the truth of My Spirit.

Ephesians 4:7–8 says, "But to each one of us grace was given according to the measure of Christ's gift. Therefore he says, "When He ascended on high, He led captivity captive, and gave gifts to men."

Ephesians 4:11–13 says, "And He Himself gave some to be apostles, some prophets, some evangelists, and some pastors and teachers, for the equipping of the saints for the work of ministry, for the edifying of the body of Christ, till we all come to the unity of the faith and of the knowledge of the Son of God, to a perfect man, to the measure of the stature of the fullness of Christ."

Place grace above all things. Measure the gifts you have been given with the ability to perform all your God has intended for you. To compare your gifts with others will not satisfy Me. Receive My grace intended for you for the gifts I have given you. This will show your love and trust in who I am. There were promises made for you in heaven in addition to the holy grace that was deposited within you when you were born again. Do not allow My promises that I have given to you in My Word to become lost by not receiving what is yours. Having a rich relationship with Jesus will implant the gifts that are yours for the glory of the Trinity. Hold to that which is good and receive all I wish to give to you. Partake of all I wish to impart to you for the unity of the body so that you reach the measure of faith in the fullness of Christ.

Chapter 9
ANGELS IN OUR MIDST

Prophetic Word

There is also an antitype which now saves us—baptism (not the removal of the filth of the flesh, but the answer of a good conscience toward God), through the resurrection of Jesus Christ, who has gone into heaven and is at the right hand of God, angels and authorities and powers having been made subject to Him. (1 Peter 3:21–22)

> There is much that needs to be known concerning My angels. My children show reproach when they refer to angels as heavenly beings who only live in the kingdom above. To go beyond what is accepted as fact, there is a truth that must be heard and recognized. The promises in My Word

are promises that include the assistance of angels, who are at the command of their God.

The intellect of a worldly mind cannot comprehend the holiness of angels. My power is coming upon the earth in this time with the evidence of the existence of angels. As My ministering angels become evident to My people, the fullness of My truth will be known to all who are filled with My Spirit with eyes of faith.

As the atmosphere is holy, this will bring forth spiritual manifestations that will be brought forth by angels filled with My grace. There are times when the laying on of hands will bring about the very presence of the angel of wisdom, which is set apart for this time. The presence of Jesus will be that of a mountaintop experience, and I will accomplish that which needs to be done. My promises will be fulfilled when My children come to me with an open heart. This is a holy time for all who have chosen to come to Me, their God, for they have chosen to break the bond of the enemy who strives to come between God and all mankind. Truly I say do not presume that anything could come to block the holiness that I have desired for this appointed time upon the earth. My angels of mercy will crowd around My children and they will have eyes to see them and have spiritual focus, for it is the time for supernatural knowledge. This will guide My people to expect supernatural manifestations as they reach out to a dying world. My promises are real and true; this is My time to pour out blessings upon the people who live in My kingdom!

In Jesus Christ there is a knowledge not yet touched by some of His children, that is, a knowledge that will be rightfully theirs because they are His disciples. This comes with a reality that will be made only to those who hear His voice. My promises are real, and they will always be forthcoming. Jesus is Lord over all who continue to follow Him. This will be evident in these days of My holy angels.

Chapter 10
HAVING EARS TO HEAR

Second Peter 1:17–21 tells us about Jesus's disciples; Peter, James, and John who heard God's voice when He spoke to Jesus on the mountain. We know from Peter, James, and John's testimonies that we also can hear God's voice. If we want to know God on a personal level, we can hear His voice more clearly as we spend quality time with Him one on one. It delights His heart that we, His children, want to know Him and want to hear what He has to say to us. In Christ Jesus we have this privilege, His favor, to know Him and acknowledge His love for us. He loves us as He loves His only begotten Son.

How very blessed are all who believe God's supernatural gifts are active and flowing in the church today as the Holy Spirit leads. Freely we have received; freely we give.

Word of the Lord

I am blowing the trumpet in Zion, calling all who have ears to hear to get ready for My holy council. Today is a day for unlimited knowledge to all who are willing to fight the good fight in the Spirit, standing for righteousness and My truth. As you stand in these times of many false gods, you stand united with all whose purpose it is to behold the King of kings and the Lord of lords, Jesus Christ. He has already conquered the battle, He is the victor, and He has won the fight.

> Every child of God has spiritual gifts Holy Spirit has fashioned for them

There should be no competition among God's people. We are all equal in who we are and who we belong to. Unity is joining together with sisters and brothers in Christ where we are planted, to move with action with one another calling those things that are not as though they were. As we pray without ceasing, the Holy Spirit will reveal to us the needs for the day in our personal lives and the world. Each day God gives us eyes in the Spirit to see how the Holy Spirit is calling us to pray. This is one reason we are to seek God's voice for ourselves and others. God is calling us to use our authority in Christ to take back what the enemy has stolen.

The light of Christ overrides the darkness. The world is getting darker, but God's glory is getting brighter. These are the days of the Lord, the season of refreshment in a world tangled in confusion, hate, and disappointment. We must remember we are God's people, a nation unto itself under the protection of a mighty God who cares for all who live in His kingdom. God wants to impart to you today a refreshing touch of His Spirit.

There is no gap between you and our Heavenly Father. Jesus filled that space, and you have crossed that bridge, making the journey to God's kingdom in and through Jesus Christ. Jesus wants to reassure you that you are loved and that you will never be forgotten. God's grace covers you, protects you, and clears the path before you. His glory will shine, and His name will be exalted. He is holy and true to His people forever.

These are truly the days of Elijah. We are declaring the word of the Lord and walking in obedience to the call. Father God does not call us to perform but to walk hand-in-hand with Him as He speaks to us with sincere intimacy, which will direct us in our walk with Him in and through His Holy Spirit. What a privilege it is for us to hear God's voice and to know His Spirit lives inside us to guide us in so many ways. How often do we think of the holiness of being able to hear God's voice?

This is a defining time for the church, a time to say yes and a time to completely surrender to the Holy Spirit's prompting to follow God's voice for our destiny. Each one in the body of Christ has a call from God that is distinct to our personality, our character, the way God designed us when He created us.

We are unique; our days were fashioned for us before God created us when we were but a desire in His heart. How awesome is this? How can we grasp the fullness of what this means? Each one of us hears God's voice the way He knows we will understand. No two people are alike. We were born to hear God's voice—His still, small voice. When we seek Him, there is no way we will miss our destiny.

Psalm 139:13–18 says: For You formed my inward parts; You covered me in my mother's womb. I will praise You, for I am fearfully and wonderfully made; Marvelous are Your works, and that my soul knows very well. My frame was not hidden from You, when I was made in secret, and skillfully wrought in the lowest parts of the earth. Your eyes saw my substance, being yet formed. And in Your book they all were written, the days fashioned for me, when as yet there were none of them. How precious also are Your thoughts to me, O God. How great is the sum of them. If I should count them, they would be more in number than the sand; when I awake, I am still with You.

Do not labor for the food which perishes, but for the food which endures to everlasting life, which the Son of Man will give you, because God the Father has set His seal on Him. Then they said to Him, What shall we do, that we may work the works of God? Jesus answered and said to them, this is the work of God that you believe in Him whom He sent (John 6:27–29).

What Is God Calling You to Do?

"He has shown you, Oh man what is good; and what does the Lord require of you but to do justly, to love mercy, and to walk humbly with your God." (Micah 6:8) I am sure you will agree that we need to seek Him fervently, deeper and deeper, with intensity. When we open our spiritual ears to hear His voice, He pours out His love just when we need His direction and His presence.

God is giving this word to you who have come with hungry hearts for more of God, more of His love, which conquers all.

Word of the Lord

To you, My beloveds, I ask you to walk with Me today with expectancy in your hearts. It is a time of My holy fire to burn throughout My church. It is a time when hearts will become ignited with the fire of the Holy Spirit who will pour new wine into the hearts of My people who hunger for more. This is a time for the l to be saved as in the days of Acts, a time for those who have gone astray to hear their Shepherd's voice to come home, a time for the Holy Spirit's boldness to overtake the fear of man. I call this a time for all people to understand with more clarity the difference between evil and good, right from wrong. This is a time when the spirit of indifference will be cast out of all who are willing to surrender their hearts fully to Jesus Christ. This is a time when My people, who seek My face, will gather to be a comfort for one another, and all will know they belong to the family of a mighty God by the love you share with one another. I ask of you, My beloveds, to come away with Me and receive My love and to share your heart with Me, your God, as I share with you how much you mean to Me.

I am the potter and you are the clay in My hands. If you are in the hands of a mighty God, how can anyone change what I have called you to be in your life? Come to Me all who are heavy laden, and I, your Redeemer, will give you rest.

Having Ears to Hear

God is awakening His people in this season. He is getting our attention to go forth to a dying world,a world that needs His love. He is calling His church to go forth and use the gifts He has given them. Every born-again believer in Jesus Christ is filled with the Holy Spirit. He is the one who brings forth the supernatural gifts and talents God created in every child of God.

This is the time, this is the day, this is the hour to dare to believe, daring to step out in faith as the Holy Spirit leads and directs us to be a witness to the unsaved, and to be an encouragement to our brothers and sisters in Christ. God is calling us to reach out to the unsaved that live in a world of devastation and brokenness. This is the time to renew hope for all who need an encouraging word from God who loves them with an everlasting love.

Chapter 11

GOD IS CALLING HIS CHURCH TO A GREAT AWAKENING

I received these prophetic words regarding God's holy revolution and the great awakening of the church from 2014 to 2018.

Prophecy: October 2014
Micah 6:8; Psalm 118:19

> How can the church change the world if there is not unity, a coming together that will procure a righteous peace with heaven coming to earth? There is a violent storm raging on the earth in stages that are uncontrollable in the minds of man. The power of man has

lost sight of the meaning of the pursuit of happiness and its necessity to live peaceably with all men.

I have called together all who are willing, all who are in pursuit of a stable world that draws hearts and minds to the intensity focused on preparing the way for the return of the Lord. How can one meet such a requirement that will draw a holy revolution to the height of the intensity that will cover the earth? To what will be the end result and how will it show the glory of the almighty God whose desire is to pour His love on all of His creation?

My Son Jesus came to demonstrate the love of His Father, the truth of how righteousness reigns over the earth in and through the power of the authority given to Him. He died for all mankind to save the world from sin and devastation. As I speak to you, My people, to join together in this revolution, it is with My peace and love I draw you nearer to My heart, to seek Me in this holy pursuit as the Holy Spirit leads you and to walk in My Spirit is to be drawn into what I have called My church to enter into for such a time as this. You may ask the question about what is so different now about pursuing My kingdom in a world that is making its own way.

The answer to you, My beloveds, is for you to consider the times you are living in today. Consider the upheaval of even those things that have been called absolutes, to walk in a morality that honors a God of goodness and not evil. I have brought to light what I require all creation, to act justly, to love mercy, and to walk humbly with their God.

I am all power and authority and have considered the times that have brought regrets to My heart, but I have called to them who walk uprightly with their God for such a time as this to go forth with a sound that is audible to all who are hungry for a God of mercy and kindness. My greater glory will rest on My people to resonate the sound of

My greater glory. This is not for the fainthearted, but for those who are willing to sacrifice a deeper surrender to the full measure. Therefore, all who have made a commitment to their Redeemer, Jesus Christ, who lives and reigns in their hearts forever, will walk in these last days with My light shining with them and before them. Did I not say in My Word the knowledge of My glory will cover the earth as the waters cover the sea? Is it not time for My people to take the kingdom of God by force? My force is not the demanding force of fear that the world brings, but a violent force of love, power, and a sound mind of virtue and contentment that brings peace and a new hope.

I look upon each and every one of My beloveds as stewards of My kingdom, knowing I have called them to be making a way where there seems to be no way. I see your hearts that are ready for the new day of My light to shine even brighter in the dark places; the light of Christ shines the light of the King of glory. The gates are open for you, the righteous, so continue to walk in My light as My Spirit guides you in peace, which is your inheritance in My Son, Jesus.

Prophetic Word: June 11, 2015

The silence over My church has caused My beloveds, who are radically in love with Jesus Christ, to break forth with an exuberance that will cut through the words of the naysayers in the church. I hold the key to this time of My great awakening in My church, and I say today is the day the lock is turned and the door is opened to this season of My promises to a dedicated people of My heart.

When I call from My mountain, the echo of My voice reaches all who are willing, all who are treading the waters of My river. I say, move into action and go with the flow, for I am stirring up My river of love, My river of extreme motion, that will cause a radical outbreak of My love through all who are surrendered without holding back, all who are willing to step into this time of breaking through the silence that has held My glory to a minimum. I call My own, My beloveds, who know My heart to listen for My voice in every part of their lives, for I am speaking loudly, and you will hear clearly if your eyes are on Me, on My Son Jesus, as I move in this time through the wind of My Spirit.

Prophetic Word: March 4, 2016

I am causing My church to awaken from a deep sleep, one that has lasted for a season but will no longer be deaf to My calling. The church is hearing the call of My trumpet in Zion, calling My people who are called by My name to awaken for the holy revolution that is for now, the time I have called to be a great awakening of the Spirit of the living God!

You, who are in the hearing of My voice, have started to walk in this time of a great shaking, a great awakening. The time of slumber in My church is over. I have caused a spark of the fire of My glory to catch and ignite, to spread throughout the land, to go forth beyond the walls of My church. I am God who was and always will be; when I speak, the mountains shake; when I send a hush to the seas, they become still. When I open the floodgates of heaven to rain upon My people, there is a gush of heavenly rain that pours out to overtake the enemy and make still the defiance of the world's unbelief. I have in My hand, ready to pour out, a multitude of unending promises. What I give, I do not take back unless eyes are turned from Me, away from who I am, Creator of all things. I am God, and there is no other.

I do not come to destroy or make havoc but to rain upon the earth with a gentle washing of things that should not be, reversing the wrong and making it right. I am causing My church to rally together, to join old and young alike, for this is My holy revolution. I am causing this to be for this hour, this season, for such a time as this. The shift has begun; the focus of My people shall be *increased with a mighty passion to walk as the redeemed of their Lord and Savior Jesus Christ who lights the path of His disciples with His Words of new life. He is the restorer of the breach by the commitment of all who carry His name in their hearts.*

These are the days of Joel, My prophet, who heard as My wisdom filled His Spirit. The voices of My prophets will be heard in louder proclamation than ever before. I am opening the ears of My people as well as their eyes, for all who are willing will see how good their God can be.

Romans 13:10–12 says, "Love does no harm to a neighbor; therefore love is the fulfillment of the law. And do this, knowing the time, that now it is high time to awake out of sleep; for now our salvation is nearer than when we first believed. The light is far spent, the day is at hand."

Ephesians 5:14 says, "Awake, you who sleep, arise from the dead, and Christ will give you light."

Follow HIS WAY, *Hear* HIS VOICE

Prophetic Word: April 29, 2016

Be glad then, you children of Zion, and rejoice in the Lord your God; for He has given you the former rail faithful, and He will cause the rain to come down for you, the former rain, and the latter rain in the first month. The threshing floors shall be full of wheat, and the vats shall overflow with new wine and oil.

"So, I will restore to you the years that the swarming locusts have eaten the crawling locusts, the chewing locusts, My great army which I sent among you. You shall eat in plenty and be satisfied, and praise the name of the Lord your God, Who has dealt wondrously with you; and My people shall never be put to shame. Then you shall know that I am in the midst of Israel; I am the Lord your God and there is no other. My people shall never be put to shame. And it shall come to pass afterward that I will pour out My spirit on all flesh; your sons and your daughters shall prophesy, your old men shall dram dreams your young men shall see visions. And also, on My menservants and on My maid servants I will pour out My Spirit in those days." (Joel 2:25–29)

Comparing this scripture to this day and time is bringing revelation that will bring confirmation, for I am leading My people into this time to be not only adequate but revelatory to what is happening. My latter rain brings My harvest to full blossom. All that it touches that has been dry, that has been delayed, and that has had growth in the former rain but was stilled in their growth because of the dryness of My Spirit in the church will be renewed.

My latter rain is falling on My church; it spills over to the streets into the dark places. My people carry My glory, which is My rain of superior wetness and not like the rain from the clouds but My glorious rain that is meant to fall for this time and season.

Time is in My hands. I decide when My rain shall fall, not man. See the signs of the times; hear the words of My truth from My prophets. Most of all, I ask My church to open their hearts to what they are sensing in their spirit. It is time to reap for My kingdom; the harvest is ripe. Go and gather for the time is near.

Prophetic Word: June 6, 2017

Isaiah 60:1–5 says, "Arise, shine; for your light has come! And the glory of the Lord is risen upon you. For behold, the darkness shall cover the earth, and deep darkness the people; but the Lord will arise over you and his glory will be seen upon you. The Gentiles shall come to your light, and kings to the brightness of your rising. Lift up your eyes all around, and see: they all gather together, they come to you; your sons shall come from afar, and your daughters shall be nursed at your side. Then you shall see and become radiant, and your heart shall swell with joy; because the abundance of the sea shall be turned to you, the wealth of the Gentiles shall come to you."

Surely this is My time that comes to cover My people, My church, as a tidal wave of My righteousness. Even as you have called upon My name, I have put on you My coat of glory. For you shall carry My glory to the ends of the earth, and My glory shall cover the earth. Even as there is a shaking going on in the earth, I am also shaking My church to awaken them to see the light of My glory. My spirit is speaking to all who know Me through

My Son; yes, He is speaking in every language, in every nation, for I am speaking to each heart that belongs to Me. My Spirit is searching for hearts in those who will be a part of my army to bring in the harvest of souls in these last days.

> Holy Spirit is holding counsel with everyone who has ears to hear what the Spirit is saying. There is nothing that will hold you back, My beloveds, for I carry you in the palm of My hand. Who could be against you if I, the living God, am for you? This is a time that has never been before in the history of the church, for it is a vital time, a time when My people, called by My Name, shall walk with Me in order to fulfill the words I have spoken for such a time as this. Many scholars have tried to name the time and the date of the revelations I have spoken of in My Word, but it is I, the Creator of all things, who will bring about what is to happen in My time only. Yes, you can see the signs of the times and this, My beloveds, is for you to know the time is near.

I call each one by name to walk out their destiny as I have called it to be. This is a time when the gathering of the saints will not only be necessary but vital for what I am bringing about. As there are many facets to a diamond, My light shines through you in many ways, for the light of My Son cannot and will not be dimmed in these days of My glory.

Therefore, this is the time you, My people, need to recalibrate your walk with Me. You hold My words in your hearts, and this is your confirmation of the love I have for you. The evil one will not prevail against you for what I have declared to you will surely be what I will do. I cover you in My secret place for it is under the shadow of My wings you will rest!

You will hear many predictions even from my most prominent prophets. I ask you to weigh out every word, to discern it even by My Spirit. I will bring confirmation to the words I speak, so weigh each message in the *truth of My Word that I have given you. In this time in the church, an echo is likened to hearing the voices of My people; it is as an echo from the highest mountaintop, an echo that never ceases, never ends, for it is an act of worship from each heart from every nation and will open the spiritual ears of many. My seeds of righteousness are being spread throughout the world through you, My beloveds; the seeds I have placed in your spirit will never run out, so I ask of you to continue to walk with the light of My Son that shines before you. My hand is upon you, and you will continue to see My glory as you keep your eyes on Me. I ask you, My beloveds, to be aware of the promises I have given you, for this is My time to pour out to you whatever is needed to restore your faith, your hope, and your trust. I am your God of wholeness to replenish all those things you feel have been lost; this is a time to put your trust in Me—your God.*

"Ask, and it will be given to you; seek, and you will find; knock, and it will be opened to you. For everyone who asks receives, and he who seeks finds, and to him who knocks it will be opened." (Matthew 7:7–9)

Prophetic Word: April 11, 2018

"I will lift up my eyes to the hills from whence comes my help? My help comes from the Lord, who made heaven and earth. He will not allow your foot to be moved; He who keeps you will not slumber. Behold, He who keeps Israel shall neither slumber nor sleep. The Lord is your keeper; the Lord is your shade at your right hand. The sun shall not strike you by day, nor the moon by night. The Lord shall preserve you from all evil; he shall preserve your soul. The Lord shall preserve your going out and your coming in from this time forth, and even forevermore." (Psalm 121:1-8)

Can you, My people, take these words to heart? Can you believe beyond the doubt that tries to creep into your mind? Could there be a time, like this time, like this season that you, My church, hear My cry to seek Me more, to seek My face in this My time of My glory? This is a time for you not to lose heart but a time for you, My people, to be anxious for nothing but to be thankful and rejoice, for it is My time for the latter rain.

I am calling you to enter into this time of the outpouring of My love that will bring forth that which I have imparted deep within you through My Spirit that will not only change your lives for the better but also all those around you that you touch with My anointing. You will see, in these days, I have called for the gathering of My people whose main purpose is to worship Me in Spirit and in truth.

My promises are not weak but strong in who I am, the almighty God who does not go back on His Word. As you depend upon My strength, you will reach the heights I have called you to, and you will be who I have called you to be in Christ, My Son. These are days of My glory, yes, but these are days I expect My church to be holy as I am holy. Time is ticking away, and all time is in My hands, so I ask you, My people, to consider your time to be used as My Spirit directs and enables you to go forth and be a witness to what your Lord has done for you. As I have called you to be ambassadors, I also called you to be listeners to what others have to say in regard to their needs. I hear every word, I see every action, and I hear their cries. I see their bleeding hearts, and I care for their every need. My fountain of love will flow over everyone you touch with My compassion and love that lives within you.

My beloveds, you are My people, a holy nation that I have called unto myself; My mercy and My grace are with you always. I ask you to renew your minds in My Word for it is My truth. I call you to believe and expect what you are asking for, and it will be given to you in great measure.

I do not want this time of My glory to be wasted. Each one of My children is gifted as I have chosen to give. Mantels and callings are being refreshed and renewed. As your heart is fully surrendered, you will go forth in My glory.

Mountains will crumble before you, mighty exploits in the name of Jesus will be multiplied, and His name will be exalted. Therefore, My glory will be spread among the people. You, My church, are being fully awakened for this day of My glory. You, My people, must go forth to awaken those who are still asleep, walking as dead men, for they do not know their God is alive. I have created all hearts to hear, but their ears must be open to what the Spirit is saying. To follow My Son, there must be true repentance and a willing heart to follow His voice. There is still time to reap the harvest, but time is short. Go forth with words of life that call all to live with Me in eternity.

Prophetic Word: June 27, 2018

Ephesians 1:3 says, "Blessed be the God and Father of our Lord Jesus Christ, who has blessed us with every spiritual blessing in the heavenly places in Christ."

My church has entered into the heavenly realm of My glory. In this season that I have called forth, that which is of My glory will be truly an expression to the world that I am God and My Son is alive.

I am shining My glory through those who have reverence for My Son who is alive and represents who I am, a God of love and mercy. My Spirit is speaking to the church in a loud voice that echoes from My heart to come closer to your Father who loves you. I am raising up those who feel they are dead in My Spirit and will cause them to come alive for who they are in Me and who I have called them to be. I am awakening even those who are downtrodden. They will find that spark of My Spirit that lives in their hearts through the resurrection of My Son and come alive to seek Me as never before. I am pouring out My mercy upon all who have been persecuted and have felt fearful because of the hate that lurks in the world. If there is just a small remembrance of who I am, their God of salvation in Christ, I shall rescue and comfort them, for I am their God *who will never leave or forsake all who call Me their God and Father.*

This is My time for great exploits that will reveal a merciful God and a loving Savior. Families will be brought back together, and there shall be respect again in this nation for the values of absolutes, which know good from evil. Even as you, My people, are hearing this, you are saying can this be? Can my God do such a thing? I say this to you My beloveds, I am God, and there is no other; I am the Creator and can do as I have created in My way and My will. My Spirit is blowing across all nations, calling all to receive My love. If I can breathe into man My breath that is My Spirit, I can breathe again to call all who want to know their God and make them alive again. I spoke to the dry bones in the valley. I am speaking again to the dry bones not only to My church but to all who have breath. All who will respond with adoration to who I am will be changed and live their lives according to My will and My way. Am I saying all will come in; all will recognize who their God is? As hearts are open to believe, they will receive new life in who I have created them to be. The message of My love must go forth and be spread to all people; it is time to spread the Great Commission through every possible communication the world has provided.

My beloveds, this is what I am asking: Seek Me in prayer and intercede for what I am doing in this, My season of glory. Do not allow the authority that you carry through My Son to be dormant but pray as My Spirit is leading you to pray without ceasing.

First Thessalonians 5:16–18 says, "Rejoice always, pray without ceasing, in everything give thanks; for this is the will of God in Christ Jesus for you."

Prophetic Word: August 3, 2018

In all that is good, all that is righteous, in My name I am calling My beloveds to see Me in the light of who I am and who I am calling them to be. The flow of My Spirit is calling forth a time for in-depth knowledge. It is time for My people who know My heart and My ways to be aware of the signs of the times, understanding spiritual insight by the leading of My Spirit. This is a spiritual awakening that will untangle that which has caused a division between man and My Spirit, the true meaning of a gathering of the saints who are seeking more wisdom of who I am and My Son, who came to save all who know his Name that is holy. There is a blanket of conviction hovering over this nation for those who have chosen to overlook evil and ignore what is blatantly false, putting evil out of their minds and calling justice a rule that is not a serious consequence. I am sitting judges in the seats of vacancy who know My heart and seek My ways of justice. I am placing a plumb line in the heart of the government for the breaking of false intentions to be swept out and replaced with the values that were first set over a nation born with liberty and justice for all. I am calling forth a time of truth above lies, and there will be an upheaval that will shake the very foundation of a governing people who have ruled by the hand of man instead of the hand of a mighty God. I am stifling the mouths of those who are taunting, those who are making trouble and not peace in the streets that are crowded with evil doers who are being fooled by their own false intentions because of their godless nature. If it were truth they were proclaiming, love would be guiding their purpose not rage.

I have placed My wall of protection over My church, and there will be signs and wonders that counteract the evil one's intentions to cause harm and depletion. I say to My people to believe again with the intention to see greater exploits, for I am bringing unusual miracles that will overrule the unbelief of the world. As you, My beloveds, believe, you will receive above and beyond your heart's desires, for I am your God of more than enough.

The blood of My Son reaches all who cry out for His divine touch no matter whether it be in the gathering of the saints or in the quiet place of their prayer closet. There are no limitations to where My Spirit will go. I am omnipresent. I am removing the obstacles that have caused My beloveds unnecessary stress and heartache in their living conditions that cause a lack of peace because of financial burdens to live in a world of many demands that are above their means. I am causing the wealth of the wicked to be poured on the righteous, for time is of an essence to show My hand of generosity through My anointed ones. I am asking all to seek Me for wisdom in their daily lives as well as what is ahead, for there are many who perish for lack of knowledge. I give My wisdom freely as I give My peace when asked with a sincere heart of thanksgiving.

Philippians 4:4–7 says, "Be anxious for nothing but in everything by prayer and supplication, with thanksgiving, let your requests be made known to God, and the peace of God, which surpasses all understanding, will guard your hearts and minds through Christ Jesus."

Prophetic Word: September 12, 2018

This is My time to turn the darkness to light and to show My goodness in ways that will be pronounced in truly supernatural expression. I am turning the tide and changing that which seems depleted into multitudes that are more than enough. As you, My beloveds, keep your eyes on Me, there will be an explosion of My love that will be such an adventure in knowing who you are in Christ that there will be a rushing of the wind of My Spirit that will feed all who are hungry to know My love.

I give direction and make the way for your obedience to follow where there seems to no way to all. It is I who marks the path and marks the journey. You, My true ones, will have the victory, for it is in My plan to lift you higher from glory to glory!

There has been a shift in the Spirit that has changed the dominion from wrong to right. This, My beloveds, is calling you to step out in who I have called you to be; to hear and to know each one makes a difference as you share the love of the God you serve. My anointing is with you wherever you go, so know you change the atmosphere wherever you put your feet.

Strategies from My Spirit still mark the way for warfare victories. Where there is war, there is victory as My church depends on Me. I lead all through My Son who is the King of glory and has already won the battle.

I ask you, My church, to take your negatives and turn them into positives. Begin every day knowing My mercies are new every morning. Just as the sun rises to give light to the earth, I shine My light on your righteousness in My Son, on each and every one who carries Me in their heart. To know Me is to walk in My love for eternity. My Son has opened the door to My heart for you, and there you will stay.

Prophetic Word: October 12, 2018

"According to the word that I covenanted with you when you came out of Egypt, so My Spirit remains among you; do not fear! For thus says the Lord of hosts: 'Once more (it is a little while) I will shake heaven and earth the sea and dry land; and I will shake all nations and they shall come to the Desire of All Nations, and I will fill this temple with glory,' says the Lord of hosts. 'The silver is Mine and the gold is Mine,' says the Lord of hosts. 'The glory of this latter temple shall be greater than the former,' says the Lord of hosts. 'And in this place I will give peace,' says the Lord of hosts." (Haggai 2:5–9)

"See that you do not refuse Him who speaks. For if they did not escape who refused Him who spoke on earth, much more shall we not escape if we turn away from Him who speaks from heaven whose voice then shook the earth; but now He has promised saying, 'Yet once more I shake not only the earth, but also heaven.' Now this, "Yet once more" indicates the removal of those things that are being shaken, as of things that are made that the things which cannot be shaken may remain. Therefore, since we are receiving a kingdom which cannot be shaken, let us have grace, by which we may serve God acceptably with reverence and godly fear. For our God is a consuming fire." (Hebrews 12:25–29)

I have spoken for all to hear rightly. The day is coming for man to know who I am and how I will prevail for all mankind to recognize what I say I will do. My words spoken are true to this day, this time, and this season. I am calling all who know My name to come closer and hear what I am calling forth in these days of My glory.

I am setting ablaze the fire of My glory that will consume every heart that walks in the tune of My Spirit. To qualify for such an outpouring of who I am, there is only the necessity of a wholehearted commitment in all who know My name. The wind of My Spirit is blowing as My angels are ready to direct each and every one on the path, which will align with My plan for their destiny. This is the time to not keep the light of Christ under a bushel but to shine where you stand to help light the way for all who need new life in Him who died to make all free. This is a time to not be in fear but to stand in all righteousness, which will keep you steady, and you will not be shaken.

I am calling nations to be forever sanctified, and there will be revival for all nations that choose freedom in all things, for I am a God who loves peace and unity with all mankind. There is a rising up of the native people in all nations, for I am calling My people to have their inheritance. I hold them in My heart, for they are a people that have been forgotten.

This is a time when My people who are called by My name will gather as family, being comforted, nurtured, and encouraged with the love of their King who abides in their hearts.

I am exposing in these days of My justice the hidden lies that were kept secret in the sanctuaries that were to be holy as I am holy. Nothing is hidden from Me, for I see all things and know all things. I am cleansing My places of worship for they must be purified and ready for the great harvest that is coming forth. I am pouring out refreshment for the gifts and callings on My people, for this is a time for the exposure of the supernatural wonders to be revealed to all who have eyes to see the works of a mighty Savoir who wants to reveal His love to all who will open their hearts to Him.

As you, My anointed ones, are ready to receive, you will go forth with the abundance of My love to give to a dying world. My promises are in full bloom for all who walk with Me, talk with Me, and know I am with them. I am stirring the waters of My truth, and all who dare to believe will receive the abundance of My grace.

Prophetic Word: January 5, 2019
Isaiah 55:6-13

I am calling forth multiple connections in the body of Christ. This is My time to renew and restore lost confidence and hope that has been deferred in the hearts of My people. The blind in faith will see again as I spread new hope where there is a lack of the fruit of patience and longsuffering.

The richness of My glory is abounding, for I am calling My church to come together in unity to cause the gathering of the saints in a way that will cause a shaking, a spiritual awakening, as in taking by force that which belongs to the redeemed in Christ, the King of glory.

My staying grace never ends because of the love I have for My people. It is a time for all who believe to reunite in the power of My authority through the blood I have sacrificed through My Son.

As I speak, the redeemed will hear if they come to Me with surrendered hearts. Who will go for Me? Who will give up all to follow their King of kings? Come to Me, and I will answer you and guide you with wisdom that is hidden from the world of unbelief. As I see your hunger, I will feed you with My wisdom that will guide you and show you marvelous things through My Spirit who wants to give you what you need, and more, as you go forth in this time of My glory.

Authority has its rightful place in My kingdom. You, My beloveds, in Jesus, will go forth with eyes that see and ears that hear as you walk in the authority that is your inheritance.

This is My covenant with the redeemed in My Son, that when they are weary, I am strong. In this time, the pressures the world puts upon you will be cast down. I am changing the negative to the positive. I ask you, My beloveds, to believe with the strength of My Spirit within you. Believe who I am *in you, in My Son, for this is a time when My strength and boldness will cause you to run for Me and speak for Me. You will see mighty miracles that will cause renewal in multitudes. As I speak, hear My words of truth and see Me in these days of outpouring of My glory—the great awakening of My church. Put aside the things of the world; ask and you will receive. Walk in My Spirit, for I want to shine My light through you.*

Ending Remarks

There is no ending to what God has written in this book. God's still, small voice lives inside you. You are God's beloved child, and His love for you has a way of communicating His plans for your life.

I believe I was led by the guidance of the Holy Spirit to be the scribe for His words written in this book. I am so grateful that He uses me as His messenger. As Jesus continues to guide you on your destiny in Him, my prayer is as you follow His way, there will be an overwhelming sense of His presence. As you keep your eyes on Jesus, there is no way you will miss how He is guiding you, showing you His way.

As you meditate on the prophetic words in this book, Holy Spirit will give you what you need to hear about your life. Father God will minister to you and encourage you as you open your heart to hear. God continues to speak to each and every child that holds Him dear in their hearts. As disciples of Jesus Christ, He guides us delicately. His hand moves in every situation and in every individual, knowing every detail in our lives.

Prayer: Father God, I ask that you impart Your voice in a deeper way in everyone who desires to hear, that You draw them closer to You in Jesus Christ by Your Spirit. Flow in every part of their lives and lead them in Your way for Your glory to be seen. Amen.

About the Author

Joan Huth has been ministering in the body of Christ for over thirty years as an intercessor and in the gift of the prophetic. Joan's accomplishments include an associate degree in prophetic ministry from Bishop Bill Hamon's Ministry Training College, an associate Bachelor of Ministry degree from Wagner Leadership Institute, and is an ordained minister and graduate of Randy Clark's Global Supernatural School of Ministry. She now serves in prophetic ministry at The Barn Vineyard Church in Landenberg, Pennsylvania.

There have been many opportunities for Joan to serve in ministry. While ministering in the gift of the prophetic for most of her Christian life, she has been privileged to use this God-given gift to mentor others who desire to hear the voice of God more clearly.

Are you hungry for more of God? Be encouraged in how to energize your time in prayer. Do you want to hear God's voice more clearly? What is the prophetic and why should everyone desire to hear God's voice? Receive more revelation in scripture as you ponder over God's wisdom through His Word. Be encouraged as God speaks to the Body of Christ through the prophetic.

www.followhisway.com

CPSIA information can be obtained
at www.ICGtesting.com
Printed in the USA
BVHW032306160819
556097BV00001B/3/P

9 781545 673928